HE'S
GOD
and WE'RE
NOT

HE'S GOD and WE'RE NOT

THE SEVEN LAWS OF THE SPIRITUAL LIFE

RAY PRITCHARD

BROADMAN & HOLMAN PUBLISHERS

Nashville, Tennessee

Published by Broadman & Holman Publishers

Nashville, Tennessee

Dewey Decimal Number: 248.84

Subject Heading: SPIRITUAL LIFE

Unless otherwise stated all Scripture citations are from the NIV, the Holy Bible, New International Version, copyright © 1973, 1978, 1984 by International Bible Society; other versions cited are HCSB, Holman Christian Standard Bible, © copyright 2000 by Holman Bible Publishers. Used by permission.; NASB, the New American Standard Bible, © the Lockman Foundation, 1960, 1962, 1963, 1968, 1971, 1972, 1973, 1975, 1977; used by permission; NKJV, New King James Version, copyright © 1979, 1980, 1982, Thomas Nelson, Inc., Publishers; TLB, The Living Bible, copyright © Tyndale House Publishers, Wheaton, Ill., 1971, used by permission; *The Message*, the New Testament in Contemporary English, © 1993 by Eugene H. Peterson, published by NavPress, Colorado Springs, Colo.; Phillips, reprinted with permission of Macmillan Publishing Co., Inc. from J. B. Phillips: The New Testament in Modern English, revised edition, © J. B. Phillips 1958, 1960, 1972; GNB, Good News Bible: The Bible in Today's English Version, © American Bible Society 1966, 1971, 1976, used by permission; NLT, New Living Translation, copyright © 1996. Used by permission of Tyndale House Publishers, Inc., Wheaton, IL 60189 USA. All rights reserved.; ESV, The Holy Bible, English Standard Version copyright © 2001 by Crossway Bibles, a division of Good News Publishers. All rights reserved; and KJV, the King James Version.

1 2 3 4 5 6 7 8 9 10   07 06 05 04 03

Dedicated to

Caroline Hall
Rudyard, Montana

Thank you, Aunt Caroline, for all your prayers.

Contents

Introduction

SOMETIMES A MAP is not enough.

Not long ago I made a visit to see a patient at a veterans' hospital in a Chicago suburb. Because I had never been there before, I checked the address and room number to make sure I wouldn't get lost. It turned out that the hospital itself is like an enormous college campus. In fact, it's larger than the college I attended. There were dozens of buildings more or less haphazardly attached to each other, with very few signs, and a road system that seemed to meander hither and yon. It was easily the most confusing hospital complex I had ever visited. After a fruitless attempt to find the man I came to see, I finally (after several attempts) found someone who could help me. But of course, she couldn't find the man either. It was as if he had been stowed away in some remote corner, and the paperwork had been lost. Eventually, she determined that he was in an auxiliary unit far to the back of the property. "Just follow the road for about a mile, turn right, go past the Ronald McDonald House. You'll pass two or three buildings; just keep going and you'll find it on the corner." Once I got to the building, there was no one at the desk. In fact, the whole building seemed deserted. I eventually found the patient by trial and error, just going into one room after another.

Life can be like that sometimes. To be accurate, life is often like that. We have a map that gives us a general idea of where to go, but we need specific directions; and still we have to make the search on our own. Every person who reads this book is on a spiritual journey of one kind or another. The truth we need to know is in the Bible. This book is meant to help you focus on those things that matter most. Writing it has been an adventure that started a few years ago when I stumbled upon the First Law of the Spiritual Life: *He's God and We're Not.* All spiritual reality begins with this principle. Until you believe this and accept it, you cannot become a Christian and you cannot grow if you are a Christian. In the ultimate sense, all sin begins with the denial of this truth. Sometime later after discovering the First Law, I began thinking about putting together a short list of the basic truths of the spiritual life that undergird everything we believe, teach, and practice. Eventually I ended up with a list of Seven Laws. As you read this book, please note that the Seven Laws begin and end with God. This is crucial because he is the source and end of all things ("For from him and through him and to him are all things." Rom. 11:36). True spirituality is always God-centered.

In my real life, the life that occupies my time during the week, I pastor Calvary Memorial Church in Oak Park, Illinois. The fact that I am a pastor and that I live in the Chicago area doesn't matter except for this: Every day of my life I am trying to explain Christianity to men and women who want to know God better. This is the third church I have pastored since starting in the ministry more than a quarter-century ago, and my task has been the same everywhere. When I have preached in other countries—Haiti, Belize, Switzerland, India, Russia, Columbia, Nigeria—I have found that Christians are everywhere searching for the same thing. Centuries ago Augustine remarked that God made us for himself, and our hearts are restless until they find rest in him. That hunger to know God intimately, deeply, and personally can be found in every person sooner or later. We want to know the God who made us, and we want to know how to make life work the way God says it ought to work.

That's where the Seven Laws come in. As I study the Bible, I am amazed at a paradox that seems to jump out from almost every page. Though the message of the Bible is not difficult to discover, the Bible itself is not a simple book. As I write these words, I am in the final stages of reading through the Bible in a year, along with hundreds of people from my congregation. For me it has been an invigorating and humbling discipline. It is a discipline for me because I have tended, in the past, to read the Bible in fits and spurts, but this year I have diligently followed the suggested schedule. It is invigorating to reacquaint myself with the incredible richness of the biblical tapestry. And it is humbling to be reminded after all these years of preaching and teaching that there is much in the Bible that I still do not clearly understand.

But that is only one part of the story. As I have read through the Old and New Testaments, I have been struck again with how properly basic the message is. Our God is a wonderful summarizer. From heaven he surveyed the vast expanse of human experience and distilled his requirements into the Ten Commandments (see Exod. 20:1–17). Think about that. Ten rules that cover the whole range of human behavior and apply equally to 6 billion people (far more than that, actually, if you consider every person who has ever lived on planet Earth). When Jesus wanted to teach his followers the essence of his message, he gave them eight beatitudes (see Matt. 5:1–12). And the transforming work of the Holy Spirit becomes, in the hands of the apostle Paul, the nine-fold fruit of the Spirit (see Gal. 5:22–23). But there is more. Micah 6:6–8 says that God requires three things of those who would please him: justice, mercy, and humility. And Jesus boiled the entire spiritual life down to this: Love God with all your heart and your neighbor as yourself (see Matt. 22:36–40). That's simple and clear, isn't it? You could take a lifetime to study and meditate and still not come to the end of those two commands.

With that in mind, I offer Seven Laws of the Spiritual Life that every Christian should know. I do not claim infallibility for this list. Obviously some things could be added, and the wording could be changed. But I am convinced that all the core truths of the Christian faith fit within these seven basic "laws" of life. This book, then, will benefit anyone desiring true spiritual growth. Although it is not evangelistic, seekers will find real value because it begins where the gospel begins—with God. Perhaps its greatest use will be to spur individual believers to grow in Christ.

On a purely personal note, these Seven Laws have been hammered out in my own life over the last few years. As a pastor I often think of myself as sitting in the grandstands watching the people of God as they make their way from earth to heaven. Sometimes it is my job to cheer them in their victories. Other times I am called alongside those who have fallen or who have taken a wrong turn or who have been knocked to the ground by the "slings and arrows of outrageous fortune." As I have spent time with God's people in situations both happy and sad, I have discovered a new appreciation for life and have found deep joy in my soul.

A few months ago I celebrated my fiftieth birthday. While crossing the half-century mark, I realized that I know less now than I did thirty years ago. Back then, in my college days, I knew a great deal (or I thought I did). I could discourse confidently on any number of topics, primarily because I never let the lack of factual information stand in the way of my opinions. That's not such a bad thing, nor is it unique in the sense that most young people feel that they could conquer the world if given half a chance—and a car with a full tank of gas.

In a sense my knowledge is now both greater and smaller than it was three decades ago. But what I know, I really know. I have a handful of convictions that cannot be shaken. I would include in that short list these truths: God is good, life is short, every day is a gift, people matter more than things, fame is fleeting, this world is not my home, and even hard times are meant for my benefit. Along the way I have learned by experience that "He's God and we're not," which turns out to be the First Law of the Spiritual Life. This has become a truth that is both a solid rock and a soft pillow to my soul. I am more and more convinced that this truth is where life begins, where it must begin, and if we do not begin here, we will never find the "abundant life" Jesus promised.

One final word and we're ready to begin. I hope you'll take plenty of time as you read this book. Underline it, mark it up, and add your own comments in the margin. Along the way you'll notice that I've scattered questions throughout the text and at the end of each chapter. Please take time to think about these questions. This book is not an end but a means to an end. It is a kind of spiritual compass to help you on your journey from earth to heaven. May the study of these Seven Laws lead you closer to God. If that sounds exciting to you, then turn the page and let's get started.

Overview of the Seven Laws

Law	Response	Key Passage
1. He's God and We're Not	Admitting Our Need	Psalm 115:3
2. God Doesn't Need Us, but We Desperately Need Him	Crying Out for Mercy	John 15:5
3. What God Demands, He Supplies	Receiving God's Gift	Ephesians 2:8–9
4. What You Seek, You Find	Seeking God First	Matthew 6:33
5. Active Faith Releases God's Power	Obeying God's Call	Hebrews 11:24–27
6. There Is No Growth without Struggle	Rejoicing in Our Trials	James 1:2–4
7. What God Starts, He Finishes	Waiting in Hope	Philippians 1:6

CHAPTER 1

The First Law:
He's God and We're Not

*I*T PAYS TO KNOW the basic stuff.

It was the first day of training camp in Vince Lombardi's third year as coach of the Green Bay Packers. In the previous two years, the team had done well, winning fifteen games and a conference championship. By the force of his personality, Lombardi had taken the Packers from losers to winners overnight. Yet as practice began in July 1961, Lombardi was scared. He worried that his team had forgotten what it would take to win the championship. He decided to approach training camp as if the players were blank slates who knew nothing at all about the game they were being paid to play. So he began with the most elemental fact of all. Facing the team at the first meeting, he held up a pigskin and said, "Gentlemen, this is a football." From the back of the room Max McGee called out, "Uh, coach, could you slow down a little. You're going too fast for us."[1]

In any field of endeavor, you must make sure you've got the fundamentals nailed down. That applies to the spiritual life just as much as to professional football. Some things are so basic that if you don't know them, you are doomed to frustration. If you do know those things, however, you have a chance to succeed beyond your expectations. For the last few years I have been putting together a short list of the basic principles of the Christian life—those truths that every believer needs to know in order to have a healthy relationship with God. I wanted a short list that would take a person from their first thoughts about God all the way to heaven. Compiling this list proved to be an ambitious goal that required a lengthy personal journey that took me to all parts of the Bible. Although I am the first to admit that any such list is bound to be imperfect and subject to correction and addition, the final list I uncovered seemed so basic that I call it the Seven Laws of the Spiritual Life.

Before we discuss each law individually, let's focus for a moment on one vital observation: *The Seven Laws begin and end with God.* That is as it should be since the Bible is a book about God, and as the answer to the first question of the Westminster Shorter Catechism reminds us, "The chief end of man is to glorify God and enjoy him forever." We were made for God. We were made to know God, to serve God, to love God, and to live forever with God. As Augustine said, "Our hearts are restless until they find rest in you." We were made to glorify God; and in the act of bringing glory to him, we will enjoy him forever. And in enjoying God, we will enjoy (in the truest and deepest sense) the life he has given us.

So where does the spiritual life begin? It all starts with this fundamental truth: *He's God and we're not.* Nothing is more basic than that. All spiritual reality begins with this truth, and if we skip this or ignore it or downplay it, nothing else in this book— or in life—will make much sense.

A Biblical Safari

In order to help us grasp this truth, let's survey a number of biblical passages. The First Law is so fundamental that I might easily find three hundred verses that teach it. Here are just a few.

"But he stands alone, and who can oppose him? He does whatever he pleases" (Job 23:13). Job understands that he cannot demand anything from the Lord. In and of himself, he has no power to change his awful condition, and he can't even demand a hearing to plead his case to the Lord. God does what he wants, and Job is powerless to oppose him.

"I know that you can do all things; no plan of yours can be thwarted" (Job 42:2). This verse introduces the final chapter of Job's saga. It comes after God has given him a theology lesson and a final exam on creation, which Job flunked miserably. He couldn't answer a single question. Now thoroughly humbled, he confesses that God is all-powerful, that he does what he wants, and that no one stands against him. This confession leads Job to deep repentance for his foolish questioning of God's plan.

"Our God is in heaven; he does whatever pleases him" (Ps. 115:3). That's pretty clear, isn't it? The Lord of the universe does whatever he pleases. Whenever I read this verse, I want to stop and say, "Any questions?"

"The LORD does whatever pleases him, in the heavens and on the earth, in the seas and all their depths" (Ps. 135:6). The psalmist then goes on to list various proofs that God does what he wants: he makes clouds rise in the sky (v. 7); he struck down the firstborn of Egypt (v. 8); he sent signs and wonders (v. 9); and he struck down many nations (v. 10). The psalm concludes with a fivefold call for everyone to praise the Lord (vv. 19–21).

"Praise be to the name of God for ever and ever; wisdom and power are his. He changes times and seasons; he sets up kings and deposes them. He gives wisdom to the wise and knowledge to the discerning. He reveals deep and hidden things; he knows what lies in darkness, and light dwells with him" (Dan. 2:20–22). When King Nebuchadnezzar of Babylon had a dream he could not remember and did not understand, he eventually asked Daniel to help him. Daniel agreed, prayed to God, and the dream and its interpretation were revealed to him. The verses quoted above are part of Daniel's response of praise to God. It is God who sets up kings and then dethrones them. He orders the times and seasons. I am especially struck by the phrase "he knows what lies in darkness." God even sees the hidden things because the darkness is not dark to him.

Let's run the story forward to Daniel 4. When King Nebuchadnezzar took credit for the greatness of his kingdom, God struck him with a kind of insanity that made him think he was a beast of the field. For seven years he lived among the wild animals. When he finally turned his heart to the Lord, his sanity was restored. This is part of his public praise to God: *"Then I praised the Most High; I honored and glorified him who lives forever. His dominion is an eternal dominion; his kingdom endures from generation to generation. All the peoples of the earth are regarded as nothing. He does as he pleases with the powers of heaven and the peoples of the earth. No one can hold back his hand or say to him: 'What have you done?' . . . Now I, Nebuchadnezzar, praise and exalt and glorify the King of heaven, because everything he does is right and all his ways are just. And those who walk in pride he is able to humble"* (Dan. 4:34–35, 37). Here is a pagan king who discovered the hard way the truth of God's sovereignty. To Nebuchadnezzar's credit, he did not hesitate to speak the truth once his sanity was restored. He proclaimed that God does whatever he wants. Even the greatest human rulers are as nothing to him. No one can question what God does. Everything God does is right. And the Lord knows how to humble the proud. It would be hard to find a clearer statement of the First Law in the entire Bible.

"Oh, the depth of the riches of the wisdom and knowledge of God! How unsearchable his judgments, and his paths beyond tracing out! 'Who has known the mind of the Lord? Or who has been his counselor?' 'Who has ever given to God, that God should repay him?' For from him and through him and to him are all things. To him be the glory forever! Amen" (Rom. 11:33–36). This wonderful doxology comes at the end of Paul's presentation of the gospel as God's answer to man's sin and his presentation of God's future plans for Israel. No one could have foreseen how God would respond to human rebellion. No one gives God advice. No one can trace his path across the starry skies. God is never in debt to anyone for any reason. Everything is from him, everything is through him, and everything is to him. And he alone gets the glory.

"In him we were also chosen, having been predestined according to the plan of him who works out everything in conformity with the purpose of his will" (Eph. 1:11). This verse is one part of a long sentence that begins with the words *"Praise be to the God and Father of our Lord Jesus Christ"* in verse 3. In verse 11 Paul is praising God for choosing us in Christ according to his predetermined plan. You might translate the last part of the verse

this way: "He arranged everything so that all things are working out just as he planned a long time ago." One of the sections of the Westminster Confession of Faith says that God ordains "whatsoever cometh to pass." As Tony Evans, pastor and author, puts it, "Everything in the universe is either caused by God or allowed by God."[2] Nothing ever "just happens," and nothing is caused by someone or something outside God's control. Some things he directly causes; other things he allows to happen. But all things in heaven and on the earth and even the things that happen in hell—even the very acts of Satan—are controlled by God. Martin Luther called the devil "God's lapdog," because even he can do nothing without God's permission. Which is why Paul can declare that everything is happening just as God planned from the very beginning.

"Then I heard what sounded like a great multitude, like the roar of rushing waters and like loud peals of thunder, shouting: 'Hallelujah! For our Lord God Almighty reigns. Let us rejoice and be glad and give him glory!'" (Rev. 19:6–7). When Christ returns to the earth, the whole world will clearly know what we know right now by faith: Our God reigns.

He reigns over all things.

He reigns in every situation.

He reigns in the best and the worst that happens to us.

He reigns over his friends and even over his enemies.

He reigns in heaven, and he also reigns in hell.

He reigns over those who doubt him and deny him.

He reigns over those who follow other gods and other religions.

Our God reigns. The world does not yet see it, and sometimes we have trouble believing it because we don't always see it either. But the truth remains and will not be changed: Our God reigns.

Time to Praise the Lord!

As I stand back and consider all these marvelous verses, one fact jumps out at me and will not be ignored: *Every time the Bible writers speak of God's sovereignty, it always leads them to praise.*

He does what he pleases . . . Praise the Lord.

No one can oppose him . . . Shout for joy to the Lord.

Everything God does is right . . . Hallelujah.

How unsearchable is his wisdom . . . To God be the glory forever.

His plan is working out perfectly . . . Praise be to God.

Our God reigns . . . Let the people rejoice and be glad.

If this truth does not fill our hearts with praise, then we either don't understand what the Bible says or we simply refuse to believe it. But the truth remains whether we believe it or not. God is in charge of all things. Even when it looks like he's not ruling, he's ruling. When chaos appears, he's in charge of the chaos. When things start falling apart, he's in charge of the falling apart of those things.

Theologians call this doctrine the "Sovereignty of God." You find it on every page of the Bible. The word *sovereign* means "king" or "ruler" or "boss." God's sovereignty means that he is calling the shots in the universe. He's in charge of all things. "The earth is the LORD'S, and everything in it, the world, and all who live in it" (Ps. 24:1).

And that's what I mean by the statement: "He's God and we're not." He is the Creator, and we are his creatures. This is truly the most fundamental principle of the spiritual life. *Until you understand this and submit yourself to it, nothing in life will work right.* Every mistake you've ever made has come as a result of forgetting who's God and who's not. I believe the first sin in the universe happened because Lucifer (an angel created by God who later became Satan) forgot who was God and who was not. Isaiah 14:13–14 seems to use poetic language to describe Lucifer's very first act of rebellion against God: "I will ascend to heaven; I will raise my throne above the stars of God; I will sit enthroned on the mount of assembly, on the utmost heights of the sacred mountain. I will ascend above the tops of the clouds; I will make myself like the Most High." Note the five "I wills" of Lucifer. When any created being attempts to become "like the Most High," the only possible result can be severe judgment from God. When we decide to "play God" and run our little portion of the universe, we will not escape judgment either.

What does it mean to you to say that God is sovereign? List some of the positive and negative events that have "worked together" for good in your life.

_____

_____

_____

_____

"We know that all things work together for the good of those who love God." (Romans 8:28, HCSB)

God's Freedom

At this point I'd like to say a word about God's freedom. Although we talk a great deal about freedom, it's usually our personal freedom in view. We rarely think about God's freedom, yet that is the major point of the passages just discussed. When you come to the bottom line, God's freedom is the only true freedom in the universe. Every other "freedom" is derived from his freedom in one way or another.

The following seven short statements flesh out the meaning of "God's Freedom."

1. He is absolutely free to do whatever he wants to do.

Because God is God, he can do whatever he wants to do whenever he wants to do it. If he wants to create a planet, or a galaxy, or even another universe, he just says the word and it happens. He is truly *free* in the absolute sense of the term. This is why he announced himself to Moses as "I AM WHO I AM" (Exod. 3:14). God is eternal, self-existent, and absolutely self-sufficient. He exists entirely apart from the universe he created.

2. He has the right to deal with me any way he chooses.

By this I mean that God was under no obligation to create you or me or anyone else. Neither is he obligated to keep us alive even one more second. He is under no compulsion to save a single member of the human race. No one has a claim on God. He can do what he wants with any of us, and no one can successfully second-guess him.

3. He doesn't have to treat me the way he treats my next-door neighbor.

Many people struggle with this concept because they think that because God did something for a friend or a neighbor or a loved one, then God is bound to do the same thing for them. But it doesn't work that way. God can deliver your neighbor from cancer, but you may die of the disease. Or vice versa. Envying your neighbor because he has something you don't have is a waste of time because God treats us as individuals, not as groups. The truth is, he *might* do for you exactly what he's done for someone else—or he might do more; he might do less; he might do something entirely different. He's God. He can deal with us the way he wants.

4. He doesn't have to treat me today the way he treated me yesterday.

This principle needs to be stated carefully to avoid misunderstanding. Since God's character never changes, we know that he is the same yesterday, today, and forever. He is always gracious, always loving, always holy, and always just. His ways are always perfect. However, that doesn't mean that what happened to me yesterday is a pattern or guarantee for what will happen tomorrow. Though God's character and his love for me will never change, how that grace, faithfulness, and love is expressed varies widely from moment to moment. One day I may need a remarkable answer to prayer. The next day I may be in the valley of suffering, waiting on the Lord to deliver me. He's always the same God, but he does not display himself in my life the same way all the time.

5. *He can answer my prayers any way he chooses.*

Everyone who has prayed very much understands this truth. One night we fish and catch nothing. The next day our nets are filled to breaking. I may be in prison one night, and an angel may come to set me free. Or God may send an earthquake to deliver me. Or I may die in prison as many Christians have over the years. A loved one with a dread disease may be spared by God for several years, only to die from that disease eventually. One day I may sense God's Spirit working powerfully in my life. Another day I may plod through the doldrums. So it goes for all of God's children. Our God is infinitely creative in the way he deals with us as he brings us to spiritual maturity. There are bright days and dark nights, and both are from the Lord.

6. *He will not tolerate any rivals to his throne.*

This is one of the clearest themes of the Bible: *There is only one God, and he demands our exclusive worship.* After reminding the Jews that he had delivered them from Egypt, God made this the First Commandment: "You shall have no other gods before me" (Exod. 20:3). That's clear, isn't it? No other gods, period. God is Number One. And there is no Number Two.

7. *He is not obligated to live up to my expectations or to explain himself to me.*

This may be the most important statement regarding God's freedom. He doesn't bind himself to do what we expect him to do. As a matter of fact, God continually surprised his people in the Bible. He cast Adam and Eve out of Eden and then made garments to cover their nakedness. He sent a flood and gave Noah a rainbow. He parted the Red Sea, arranged for daily delivery of manna and quail, and then had the sons of Korah swallowed up by the earth. Jesus rebuked Peter, allowed him to see the Transfiguration, predicted his betrayal, restored him, and then predicted the way he would die. Everything happened just as God promised, but nothing worked out the way people expected. He's the God of great surprises.

And he doesn't have to explain himself to us. There are many questions we would all like to ask. I have a handful of my own. Almost always our questions revolve around suffering, sadness, the death of loved ones, and times of personal disappointment. I have found that the greater the sadness, the less likely we are to fully understand it. Small things we can figure out on our own; great losses are hidden in the mind and heart of God. "The secret things belong to the LORD our God" (Deut. 29:29).

Perfect in His Perfections

God is far bigger than we imagine; his presence fills the universe; he is more powerful than we know, wiser than all the wisdom of the wisest men and women; his love is beyond human understanding; his grace has no limits; his holiness is infinite; and his ways are past finding out. *He is the one true God.* He has no beginning and no end. He created all things, and all things exist by his divine power. He has no peers. No one gives him advice. No one can fully understand him. He is perfect in all his perfections.

There is nothing we have, not even our praise and worship, that adds in the least to who God is. He did not create us because of any lack in himself, as if we were created because God was lonely. To paraphrase author A. W. Tozer, were every person on earth to become an atheist, it would not affect God in any way. The belief or disbelief of the human race cannot change the reality of who God is. To believe in him adds nothing to his perfection; to doubt him takes nothing away.

Suppose you were allowed to ask God three questions about things that have happened in your life. What would you ask him?

1. _____

2. _____

3. _____

"To God belong wisdom and power; counsel and understanding are his." (Job 12:13)

Time Is God's Brush

God rules all things everywhere at all times. Nothing escapes his notice. Nothing is beyond his control. He is beyond time and space, yet he controls them both. Author Ravi Zacharias put it this way: "Time is the brush with which God paints his story on the canvas of human history. Eternity is the perspective from which we view the painting."[3] This is our God!

As we consider who God is, we are eventually led to a very humbling truth, one that is not mentioned often and is hardly believed when it is taught: *God does not need us for anything.* If any concept flies in the face of contemporary American Christianity, this is it. Down deep inside, most of us want to feel that we are important and necessary. We like to think that God must have needed us, or else why would he have created us? In the absolute sense, God doesn't "need" anything or anyone. He didn't create us because he was lonely, and he didn't save us because heaven was empty. He does not need our worship or our obedience or our missionary service or our prayers or anything else we do in order to be God. There is no lack of any kind with him. This is a very humbling, and for some people a very frustrating, truth. But ask yourself this question: *Do you really think God can't get along without you?* What if your entire congregation just disappeared, poof, just like that? What if it had never even existed? Do we think the universe depends on us for its survival? Hardly. When the Pharisees told Jesus to rebuke his cheering disciples as he entered Jerusalem for the final time, he replied, "If they keep quiet, the stones will cry out" (Luke 19:40). If God wants to, he can cause the trees to clap their hands and the mountains to sing out his praises. He can make the rocks sing his praises.

That God created us is an act of his sovereign will. That we are saved is a miracle of sovereign grace. That he accepts our worship and rewards our obedience is a miracle of sovereign love.

Before going on, I should add one or two clarifying points. The intended result of the teaching just given is to destroy all human pride and to leave us lying in the dust. We must come to the place where we understand that there is nothing good in us. Apart from God's kindness, there is no reason for him to use us at all. If God "needs" us to do his work, it is only because he has ordained to work through us to accomplish his will. Because God is God, he could have set up the universe in some other fashion. We are blessed beyond measure that God allows us the honor of praising him, serving him, and proclaiming his glory to the nations.

Of course there is much more we need to know about who God is than what I have said here. The Bible is filled with rich truth about our heavenly Father. As we move through this book, we will talk a great deal about his mercy and grace. In this first chapter, however, it is crucial that we get ourselves firmly grounded in the truth of God's absolute, unquestioned, totally free sovereignty. While listening to the radio many years ago, I heard a country preacher shouting into a microphone in East Tennessee. I don't remember anything about his message except one line that he kept repeating (at an ear-splitting decibel level): "God do what he want to do!" That's terrible grammar but excellent theology. God does exactly as he pleases—all the time, everywhere, in every situation, in all parts of the universe. Always has, always will. In a profound sense, his ultimate will is always being done. He's God. That's the way it has to be.

Our Response

As I have pondered this truth of God's freedom, many applications come to mind. Properly understood, it ought to lead us to a calm confidence in God even in the midst of unspeakable tragedy. It should also make us bold in our witness and strong in our prayers. Finally, if we believe this truth, we will find the strength to persevere over the long haul, knowing that even our foolish mistakes cannot cancel God's plans for us.

While all of this is true, the core issue for us individually is: How do I respond to the truth that God is God and I am not? Every single day each of us must make a fundamental choice. We can reject this First Law and decide to fight against it, but that rebellion leads inevitably to anger, bitterness, despair, and finally to a hardened heart. I know a few believers who have chosen this path. Some end up dropping out of church altogether because they are so angry that they cannot come to worship anymore. More often in my experience, however, the people who choose this path stay in church and end up as very angry Christians. They are hard to talk to because they are secretly (or not so secretly) fighting against the Lord. Usually they have suffered an enormous personal loss and cannot find a way to reconcile what they have lost with the God they have always worshiped. Though they come to church Sunday after Sunday, sitting in the pews, singing the hymns, praying the prayers, and going through the motions, their hearts are not in it because down deep they are angry at what God has done. They have the "wounded spirit" spoken of in Proverbs 18:14 (KJV). It is very difficult to help them unless God's Spirit softens their heart.

But there is another choice we can make. If we accept the First Law as true, and if we submit ourselves to God, and if we acknowledge that he is free do what he wants to do, *that submission leads to joyful praise.* The truth of God's freedom ought to lead us to praise and worship. If it doesn't, we haven't fully understood the biblical teaching. It is not that we will praise God directly for the pain and sadness around us or for the sinful acts of others. But we will praise God that he is able to work in, with, and through everything that happens, both the good and the bad, to accomplish his will, to make us more like Christ, and to bring glory to himself. To say that is to say nothing more than what Romans 8:28 clearly teaches: "We know that all things work together for the good of those who love God" (HCSB).

Submission and Praise

One Saturday night a few years ago I was working in my office at home. My office is located in the corner of our basement so that when I'm there, I won't be bothered and I won't bother anyone else. I rarely have visitors to my home office, and no one ever drops by on Saturday night. On this particular night, however, I heard a knock at the door. When I opened it, there stood an old friend with tears streaming down his face. As he walked in and sat down, he kept repeating two words: "It's over." I knew what he meant. His marriage was coming to a very sad end. Although both he and his wife were Christians, a series of sinful choices had brought their marriage to a total collapse. That night she told him she was filing for divorce. My friend sat in my office, tears coursing down his cheeks, thoroughly broken as he realized that soon his marriage would be over and he would be divorced.

Yet he went on to say that two things helped sustain him in this agonizing personal crisis. The first one was a song that was playing on the local Christian station: "Life Is Hard but God Is Good." My friend had heard it so many times that he knew the words by heart. Now he was discovering through his pain that both parts of the title were true. Life *is* hard. No one had to convince him of that. But as he now contemplated the wreckage of a marriage he had hoped would last forever, he was realizing that even in his pain, God *is* good. In addition to the song, he said that he had learned a verse of Scripture that was helping him greatly. It was Psalm 115:3: "Our God is in heaven; he does whatever pleases him." On the surface, that might seem a strange verse for such a sad moment, yet to him it was a lifeline. *The truth of God's sovereignty and God's freedom meant that what was happening to him was part of the outworking of God's plan.* Though human sin had caused the breakup, God had allowed it to come and had not intervened to stop it. Therefore, my friend was confident that God would help him through this painful time, and that in the end, he would learn many much-needed lessons.

How would you answer someone who says, "I cannot worship a God that allows so much pain and suffering in the world"?

_____

_____

_____

_____

"But as for you, you meant evil against me; but God meant it for good. . . ." (Genesis 50:20, NKJV)

Rebellion Leads to Slavery

All of that happened a number of years ago, yet my friend would say that he believes that verse even more today than he did then. Nothing happens anywhere in the universe by accident. There is no such thing as luck or fate or chance. God is at work in all things at all times to accomplish his will in the universe. He does whatever pleases him. I understand why some people rebel against a high view of God's sovereignty. The paradox is this: *People who rebel against God usually do so in the name of freedom.* They want the freedom to go their own way; to follow their own desires; to do whatever they want, when they want, with anyone they choose. Ironically, this sort of "freedom" leads only to slavery. These individuals end up enslaved to sin, chained to addictive behaviors, locked in a personal prison of unrelenting guilt and shame. There is no freedom in rebellion against God. There is only slavery.

But when we submit ourselves to our heavenly Father, when we finally say, "Lord, you are God and I am not," when we bow before him, through our tears if necessary—then (and only then) do we discover true freedom. This is what Jesus meant when he said, "You will know the truth, and the truth will set you free" (John 8:32). Those whom the Son sets free are free indeed.

The basic problem for many of us is that *we have allowed God to be everywhere but on his throne.* No wonder we are unhappy and frustrated and unfulfilled. No wonder life doesn't work right. How much better to say with the psalmist, "Come, let us bow down in worship, let us kneel before the LORD our Maker" (Ps. 95:6). There is coming a day when "every knee shall bow . . . and every tongue shall confess that Jesus Christ is Lord, to the glory of God the Father" (Phil. 2:10–11, TLB). If that day is coming, then why not get a head start and bow your knee and confess that God is God and Jesus Christ is your Lord?

Here is a simple phrase that captures this truth: "The Lord is God, and there is no other." Can you say those words? I challenge you to say that sentence out loud right now. Make it a public affirmation of your faith.

Imitating Pastor Ray

Recently our high school ministry sponsored a "road rally." About sixty of our teenagers took part. I don't know the details except that they were divided into nine teams and sent on foot to various locations in Oak Park, where they had to find a certain person, give the password, and then at each location they had to perform a specified act. The team that made it to all the stops in the shortest time was the winner. Afterward they had a time for refreshments and testimonies at the church. I know about the event because our house was one of the stops. Between 7:30 and 9:15 that Saturday night, we had nine groups of high school students in our living room. When each arrived, they were told that one person in the group was to give his best impersonation of me preaching on Sunday morning. They all laughed when they heard about it, and there was no shortage of volunteers. Nine times I watched as the high schoolers mimicked my preaching. The funniest part was, without any prearrangement, they all did the same thing. They started by saying, "How are ya doin'? No, I mean, How are you doing?" Then they would go to one side of the living room and turn it into a timeline, just like I do on the platform on Sunday morning. They waved their hands just like I do and said things like, "This is Genesis." Then they would take a step and say, "This is where David killed Goliath." Another step and say, "And this is Goliath." Another step and say, "This is the Mediterranean Sea." And to great peals of laughter, they would go to the other side of the room and say, "This is the Book of Revelation." Finally, they came back to the middle and said, "Run to the cross!" Pretty funny because (a) that's exactly what I do on Sunday morning, and (b) all the students did the same thing. It just goes to show that even when you think young people aren't listening, they are noticing everything.

The only student who did something different was one young man who did everything I just said and then added one sentence. He made a motion with his arm like he was ripping something off his chest and said, "You can rip that 'big G' off your sweatshirt." That statement amazed me because I hadn't said that in a long time, and I really hadn't said it that often. The "big G" stands for the word *God*, and ripping it off means that you don't have to play God anymore because God is God and we're not.

And that's exactly what we all have to do. Sooner or later we all have to rip the "big G" off our sweatshirt and decide that we aren't going to try to be God any longer.

There is an old Shaker hymn that says:

'Tis a gift to be simple, 'tis a gift to be free,
'Tis a gift to come down to where we ought to be.

When we finally and fully and deeply grasp the First Law, we will "come down to where we ought to be."

"Man No Be God"

The tragedy is that it takes us so long to learn this basic truth. One of the pieces of really good news in this story is that while our first thoughts about God are often wrong, *it's never too late to change our minds*. While there is life and breath, there is always an open door for repentance and change. But we must take the first step. Greg and Carolyn Kirschner, our church's missionaries in Jos, Nigeria, wrote about the importance of prayer in the Nigerian culture. They pointed out that the Nigerians seem more naturally aware of God than most Americans. To illustrate, they described this sign they saw painted on the side of a bus: "Man no be God." That sums it up, doesn't it? None of us is God; we never were, and we never will be. The sooner we all realize that fact, the better off we'll be. And here's the good news: If you do finally accept this truth, you can take a deep breath and go rip that "big G" off your sweatshirt. You don't

> **A TRUTH TO REMEMBER:**
>
> Our basic problem is that we have allowed God to be everywhere but on his throne.
>
> ❦

have to be God anymore. *Let God be God, and all will be well.* Perhaps some of us need to say, "Oh God, you win. The battle is over. I'm going to stop fighting you." If you need to say that, do it right now. There is abundant joy for all who will admit the most fundamental truth in the universe: *He's God and we're not.* This is the First Law of the Spiritual Life.

GOING DEEPER

1. Why is "He's God and we're not" the most fundamental truth of the spiritual life? Consider the following statement: "Every mistake you've ever made has come from forgetting who's God and who's not." Do you agree or disagree?

2. In what sense does God reign over his enemies and over those who doubt him and deny him?

3. "God does not need us for anything." If this is true, then why should we serve God at all, or why should we pray?

4. Read Isaiah 40:21–31 out loud. Underline each phrase that emphasizes the sovereign power of God. Ask God to make the promises of verse 31 come true in your life.

5. In what areas are you fighting against God right now? What will it take for you to lay down your weapons, walk off the battlefield, and say, "Lord, you win. I'm not going to fight you any more"?

6. How big is your God? When was the last time you prayed for something so big, so amazing, so impossible that only God could provide it?

CHAPTER 2

The Second Law:
God Doesn't Need Us, but We Desperately Need Him

THE PHONE CALL CAME FROM A MAN I had never met. As he told me his story, he began to weep. After many years of marriage, he foolishly committed adultery. He tried to hide it, but he couldn't live with himself. For months he hid it, making excuses in a futile attempt to soothe his guilty conscience. After much inner turmoil, he finally decided to come clean. His wife hadn't suspected a thing. With his voice breaking, he said, "Pastor Ray, I thought she was going to throw me out. I thought she would tell me to pack my bags and get out. I thought she would say, 'I'm through with you.'" Then he said, "But she didn't. She told me she still loved me and wanted to save our marriage. I've never experienced anything like that in all my life." Then he went on to tell the people where he worked about what had happened. He also gave them his resignation from being a missionary. "They didn't condemn me. They put their arms around me and said, 'We want to help you. We want to see you restored.'" Then his voice broke completely. "All my life I've heard about the grace of God. But I never really experienced it until this week. Now I know that God has grace even for people like me."

If any of us wants to experience God's grace, we can—but we have to cry out for it first. Until we see how much we need the Lord, we'll never ask for grace, much less receive it. And we'll never ask for God's help as long as we think we're in control of our own lives. That's really what the First Law is all about. Until we have settled the issue of who's God and who's not, we're still in spiritual kindergarten. And as long as we fight against God's right to be God, our lives will be miserable, and we will be angry and deeply frustrated. It is only when we finally come to the place where we can rip the big G off our sweatshirt that we're ready to move on.

That brings us to the Second Law, which builds directly on the First Law.

Law 1: He's God and we're not.

Law 2: God doesn't need us, but we desperately need him.

Who God Is

As it is stated, this law first tells us about God. To say that God doesn't need us means that he is totally and truly sovereign over the universe. He's the boss, the ruler, and the Lord of all things. That means he alone has true freedom. Go to any Bible college or seminary and you will hear learned (and sometimes heated) debates about *free will.* But when we use that term, we almost always refer to human free will. Years ago I expended a lot of energy in those debates. And I was always on the side of those arguing for human free will. That seems odd to me now since the term *free will* appears nowhere in the Bible. Here's the truth of the matter: *Only one person in the universe has free will. Find that person and you've found God.* Our "free will" is drastically limited; his is not. He can do whatever he wants to do whenever he wants to do it, which is the proper definition of free will. While it is true that we humans have important moral choices to make and that God will hold us 100-percent accountable for those choices, any "free will" we have is strictly derivative. *The "freedom" we have to obey (or to rebel) is freedom that God has given to us.*

The Second Law also tells us other things about God. First of all, it alludes to God's *transcendence,* something the Bible indicates to us when it tells us that God is high and lifted up. Transcendence means that God created the universe and is separate from it. The universe is not an extension of God or a necessary part of God. He existed in and of himself long before the universe was created. This law also points us to God's *holiness.* Holiness is a hard attribute to define because it is basic to who God is. Holiness is what makes God God. It's the "Godness" of God that separates him from his creation. Holiness involves purity and separation from sin, but it goes beyond that. We might say it this way: *If God were not holy, he would not be God at all.* Finally, this law impresses upon us the truth of God's *immensity.* All power and all wisdom and all majesty reside in him alone. He inhabits all things, and his presence fills every part of the universe. There is nowhere you can go where he is not already there.

Who We Are

Not only does the Second Law tell us something about God, it also tells us something about who we are. To say that we desperately need God reveals our inherent weakness. We are sinners by birth, by nature, and by choice. The true condition of the human race is revealed in these penetrating words from Romans 3:10–12: "There is no one righteous, not even one; there is no one who understands, no one who seeks God. All have turned away, they have together become worthless; there is no one who does good, not even one." Even a casual reader is struck with the universal emphasis of these words: "no one . . . not even one . . . no one . . . no one . . . all . . . no one . . . not even one." It's hard to miss the point: *The whole human race has rebelled against God.* As a result, when God looks down from heaven, he can't find a single righteous person. Not even one. He can't even find anyone who truly seeks him. Sin has so warped the human heart that no one does anything truly good in his sight. We are all "worthless" in his sight.

That last part is a pretty tough bottom line. How can you square the word *worthless* with the fact that "God so loved the world" (John 3:16)? Why would anyone love a worthless person? The answer goes to the very heart of the Second Law: *God loves us in spite of our sin and not because of some supposed worth he found in us.* To put it in basic terms, he found nothing worth saving in us but saved us anyway because that's the kind of God he is. That thought is both humbling and thrilling. None of us deserved God's grace. If we deserved it, it wouldn't be grace at all. Any "worth" we have to God is worth that he gives to us. We have value because he values us, not because of anything in us.

Rate yourself on the following scale from 1 to 10:

1	2	3	4	5	6	7	8	9	10
Definitely a Sinner				About Average				Better than Most People	

Extra credit: How would the people who know you best rate you? Hint: Ask them!

The Second Law exposes our phony independence, our casual arrogance, our sinful pride, and our obsessive need to be in control. It tells us that we aren't in control and we weren't ever in control, not even when we thought we were.

We can find this concept in numerous places in the Bible:

- "I am the vine; you are the branches. If a man remains in me and I in him, he will bear much fruit; apart from me you can do nothing." (John 15:5)
- "What a wretched man I am! Who will rescue me from this body of death?" (Rom. 7:24)
- "The man who thinks he knows something does not yet know as he ought to know." (1 Cor. 8:2)
- "Such confidence as this is ours through Christ before God. Not that we are competent in ourselves to claim anything for ourselves, but our competence comes from God." (2 Cor. 3:4–5)

A God Greater than My Dreams

Before going on, let me pause to make a purely personal comment. *It occurs to me that thirty years ago I would not have enjoyed reading a chapter like this very much.* Too much emphasis on God and on our human weakness. In my younger days, I wanted to hear about my potential, my possibilities, and what God could do through me. As I look back, I think a lot of that came from being young and feeling invincible. And that's not an entirely bad thing. In fact, I think it's good that our young men and women dream great dreams, have high hopes, and set out to do something big with their lives. Why not? Sometimes young folks do things that the rest of us thought couldn't be done. Because no one bothered to tell them they couldn't do it (or they ignored the advice), they went out and did it. Thank God for the valiant faith of those who are in high school or college or post-college and have not yet turned thirty.

But having just reached my fiftieth birthday, I have come to have a deeper appreciation for the hard realities of life. Soon enough, today's excitement will wash up against the hard rocks of reality. Not every dream will come true. If you live long enough, you'll have to face some hard times and some deep disappointment. That, too, is from the Lord and is part of the inevitable process of growing to spiritual maturity. At this point in my life, I am more aware than ever of my own limitations. I can think of more things I can't do than I can do. I am not as impressed with my talents and abilities as I used to be. So it goes for all of us. And in place of those things, I find myself increasingly glad that we worship a God whose power is unlimited, who never grows weary, whose plans will not be defeated, and whose ways are far beyond our own. What a comfort to serve a God like that.

I need a big God, a God who is almighty, all-powerful, all-knowing, and all-wise. I need a God who is the Rock of Ages. My wife and I learned this several years ago when our youngest son, Nick, came home from school saying that one of his gym teachers had noticed bruises all over his body. We had seen some of the bruises ourselves; but since Nick was a football player, we assumed it was nothing unusual. Nick had just turned sixteen and looked to be the picture of health. He was in the best shape ever after working out all summer preparing for the football season. He was 6 foot 2 inches tall and 195 pounds of pure muscle. It didn't seem likely that anything could be wrong with him, but we decided to take him to the doctor as a precaution. The doctor took a look, ran a few tests, and said he would call us with the results.

The next day I was at my office when Marlene called to say that Nick's test results revealed a serious blood problem and the doctor told us to get Nick out of class (he was a sophomore in high school at the time) and take him directly to the emergency room at West Suburban Hospital in Oak Park. It turned out that his blood platelet count was dangerously low. The cause was unknown, but since the platelets cause the blood to clot, if the situation was not stabilized, we were told that he could begin to bleed internally. After admitting him, the medical team ran a vast battery of tests that revealed a number of problems with his immune system.

To say that our lives changed at that moment is an understatement. Nick was finished with football. He started taking high doses of steroids in an attempt to raise his platelet level. We started weekly visits for testing. He had almost daily massive nosebleeds—sometimes fifteen minutes long. Many times he would get up in the morning and find his pillow saturated with blood. At one point his bleed time (how long it takes for blood to clot) was more than an hour. (Normal is two to eight minutes.) The doctors told us that Nick had a rare condition called Evans Syndrome. Over the next few months we took Nick from one specialist to another to make sure we had an accurate diagnosis. We talked to everyone we knew, found an Internet discussion board for Evans Syndrome patients, and began reading and learning about blood components and autoimmune disorders.

"Everyone has dying children."

We talked, we prayed, and we cried. At one point Marlene and I lay in bed crying because of the reality that Nick could die. We did our best to turn him over to God daily and trust him for Nick's life. In fact, it happened that during that time I was preaching a series called "Conversations with Jesus." One of my messages was titled "Jesus Speaks to the Father of a Dying Son" (based on John 4:43–54). That topic had been chosen and scheduled months before Nick became ill. Marlene told me later that while I was preaching, she had a deep sense that God was speaking to her and saying, "Everyone has dying children. You are just more aware of it at this time."

Eventually the steroids didn't work, so the doctors tried a different treatment that cost ten thousand dollars each time they used it. When that failed, they resorted to chemotherapy to force the blood platelet count up. That worked, but it wasn't a long-term solution. The last hope seemed to be the removal of his spleen. Although they feared Nick could bleed to death on the operating table, the doctors felt that a splenectomy offered the best chance for regaining his health. The problem was complicated by the fact that Nick was eventually diagnosed as having two extremely rare blood disorders—Evans Syndrome and Antiphospholipid Syndrome. One doctor told us bluntly that autoimmune disorders cannot be cured and that Nick should prepare to live with his medical condition for the rest of his life.

As soon as word got out about Nick's situation, the people at church began praying for him. We took Nick to the elders for prayer. Other people around the country began praying for Nick. Marlene and I prayed together often, but I must admit there were many times when I could not form intelligent prayers. I wasn't sure what to pray. I have a deep, settled belief that prayer works and that God answers prayer; but I believe as deeply that God is not obligated to answer our prayers the way we want him to. So, there were many times I truly did not know how to pray. But almost daily we heard of people praying for Nick.

The night before surgery we went to the hospital for pre-admission tests and a CAT scan. When he completed his CAT scan a nurse told us the doctors had decided to admit him because his levels were not good and they would need to give him treatment during the night. He had also developed a fever. There was a possibility surgery would be postponed. We were devastated. It had been difficult to organize the platelet donors, Nick was emotionally ready, and the date worked well because of spring break so he wouldn't have to miss too much school. We didn't want to put it off any longer.

Shortly after Nick was admitted, Marlene called the chairman of our elder board to ask the elders to pray. We later found out that not only the elders prayed but that most of our congregation also prayed—some having been notified two or three times. The doctors decided to wait until morning to give Nick a special drug to boost his platelets. Nothing was given to him during the night, but for the first time since he was diagnosed six months earlier, his platelets rose for "no reason." But we knew the reason. God answered the prayers of his people.

Nick was taken to surgery and in less than two hours the doctor came to tell us Nick had done remarkably well. He lost less than one-half cup of blood in a surgery that can be very bloody. The doctor told us it reminded him of a plaque his father had on his wall—"Trust God and Row to Shore." He remarked, "I did the rowing, and God did the rest."

Nick's blood platelet count improved immediately after surgery, and in the nearly two years since then, his various blood numbers have remained strong. The disease is not gone, but right now Nick is in a period of good health. He started lifting weights again and played football during his senior year. What is his prognosis? We don't know. Every patient with these rare disorders responds differently. He could wake up tomorrow in crisis, but for now things are good. We try to keep a close eye on his physical condition, and we take one day at a time.

We're Not in Control

The only way we were able to get through those really awful months was through the prayer support of God's people. I know many people asked for Nick's complete and total healing. I truly believe God could have done that, but for some reason he chose not to do that yet. Still, I think it was truly miraculous the way God daily enabled us to function, to keep living, to keep working, to keep believing that he was good and that everything in our lives happens for a purpose. God used his praying people to encourage us. Not long ago Marlene and I traveled to both Atlanta, Georgia, and Schroon Lake, New York. In both places, people we did not know asked, "How is Nick? We have been praying for him." What a wonderful, humbling experience. These people had never met Nick, but they had heard about his situation and had been impressed by God to pray for him.

Looking back I can see God's hand before and during the entire ordeal. Day to day the process was not easy; in fact, there were many desperate times. But God was there each day working in the circumstances. As I write these words, we are two years past this crisis, and all seems to be well. Not long ago, however, I was reminded that we are still completely vulnerable. I had traveled by myself to a distant state to speak at a Bible conference. Just after 4 A.M. I was awakened by a call from my wife saying that Nick had developed tremendous pain in his upper leg and she was taking him to the hospital emergency room. The doctors had told us after his surgery that one lingering effect of the Antiphospholipid Syndrome could be blood clots that could show up without warning. As Marlene and I talked on the phone, we both felt the old fear returning. We prayed together, and after I hung up I tried to go back to sleep; but the "what ifs" of the situation kept me awake. Blood clots are serious business. People die from clots that break off and go to the heart or the lungs. A thousand foreboding thoughts ran through my mind as I lay in the darkness far from home. It would be many hours before I heard from Marlene again. In the meantime, I had to preach twice and try to maintain my composure. Later she called to say that Nick was home and the pain had subsided somewhat. A battery of tests failed to reveal the source of the problem. Was it a clot that appeared and then suddenly dissolved? Was it a severe bruise? Was it something else? We do not know. That morning when I preached, I told the audience that I was learning again how much I need the Lord and how little of life is really in my control.

Nick is doing well today, and we take life one day at a time. We all understand that the line between joy and sorrow is very thin indeed. Sometimes life reminds us forcibly that we aren't in charge of anything, and we never were.

I conclude from all of this that I need a God who is bigger than all my problems. I need that God, and I need him more than I know. I *desperately* need God. Sometimes I feel my need; often I don't. But feelings don't matter in any case. I desperately need the Lord. And so do you. So do we all.

Can you think of a difficult time in your life when you learned how desperately you need the Lord? How did that experience change your life?

_____

_____

_____

_____

"I waited patiently for the LORD; he turned to me and heard my cry. He lifted me out of the slimy pit, out of the mud and mire; he set my feet on a rock and gave me a firm place to stand."
(Psalm 40:1–2)

From Theology to Praise and Worship

Let me summarize the Second Law in several succinct statements:

1. God is free to do whatever he wants to do whenever he wants to do it.

2. God was not obligated to create us, and he is not obligated to save us.

3. Everything God does for us is an act of sheer sovereign amazing grace.

4. Therefore, we are continually in his debt at all times.

5. That thought should lead us to praise and worship as a way of life.

The Second Law is not simply a statement of theology. It's meant to be *a crucial stepping stone in the spiritual life.* First, you admit that God is God and you are not. Then you confess your utter and complete need for God's help. Until you can say that from your heart, you are not yet to first base on your spiritual journey.

There are many places in the Bible that teach this truth. As I pondered the Second Law, my mind was drawn to Psalm 100. Many years ago this psalm was sung to a tune called "The Old Hundredth." Today we know the tune better as the "Doxology." You can find a musical version of Psalm 100 in most hymnals, usually under the title "All Creatures That on Earth Do Dwell." The Hebrew text calls it "a psalm for giving thanks." Even though there are many thanksgiving psalms, this is the only one specifically titled that way. It is also sometimes called the "Jubilate," which means "Oh be joyful." In Old Testament times, the Jews used it as part of the temple worship. These simple words have blessed the hearts of God's people for nearly three thousand years.

He Is God and He Is Good

Psalm 100 has two stanzas, and each is centered around God. We are to give thanks and praise the Lord because

- he is God (vv. 1–3), and
- he is good (vv. 4–5).

Verse 3 says, "Know that the LORD is God." Other versions say, "Know that the LORD, He is God" (NKJV), which makes it even more pointed. This acknowledgment of God's sovereignty leads to three corporate responses:

We shout for joy (v. 1).

We serve the Lord with gladness (v. 2a).

We sing with joy (v. 2b).

Then there is a statement of ownership and assurance: "It is he who made us, and we are his; we are his people, the sheep of his pasture" (v. 3b). Some versions say, "It is He who made us, and not we ourselves" (NKJV). I actually prefer that translation because it emphasizes that there are no self-made men or women. All that we have was given to us by God. After I shared this truth with my congregation, someone asked me if that statement applies to a man like Hugh Hefner, the multimillionaire founder of the *Playboy* empire. The answer is yes; he was given certain gifts, talents, and opportunities by God. The fact that he has badly misused them does not change the fact that they came from God in the first place.

Wanted: More Public Praise!

This leads us on to visible, public thanksgiving and praise: "Enter his gates with thanksgiving and his courts with praise; give thanks to him and praise his name" (v. 4). The design of the tabernacle and the temple allowed for large courtyards where great crowds of people would gather. The psalmist here exhorts the people to come into the courtyard singing and openly praising God's name. It's almost as if God is saying, "You want to meet me? You can. Start singing a hymn or a chorus, and I'll meet you on the second verse." Part of the emphasis is surely meant to be that Israel would publicly praise the Lord. As the pagan nations watched from a distance, the public, loud, joyful worship of the Israelites sent a message to the watching world: "These people know and love their God."

I do not think it is out of place to suggest that we Christians today should be bolder and more public in our praise. Every four years teams gather from every corner of the globe for the Olympic Games. Sometimes the team from Germany wins, sometimes it is the team from Norway or France or Australia or China or the United States. There is great rejoicing in the countries of those who win the medals. But if the people of the world celebrate an Olympic medal, which will one day melt away, how much more should we Christians openly celebrate our great God? We should praise the Lord on the street, in the parks, in the classrooms, on the job, in our offices, in our neighborhood, and with our friends and loved ones. And while we don't need to be pushy or offensive, we shouldn't be silent either. As I look at the congregation I pastor, I think we do reasonably well in this area. That is, we do pretty well for a Midwestern, middle-class, suburban congregation. We don't worship like they do in Haiti or Africa or many countries of the world where the congregation walks to church singing and chanting and laughing and lifting up the name of the Lord. We're too reserved for that. As much as I enjoy our worship services, there is room to improve in terms of joyfully praising the Lord.

His Mercy Endures Forever

Psalm 100 ends with these reassuring words: "For the LORD is good and his love endures forever; his faithfulness continues through all generations" (v. 5). Because God's mercy endures forever, it has no beginning and no end. Before time began, he was the eternal Father of Mercies; therefore, since God is eternal, his mercy extends as far into the future as the mind can conceive—and then infinitely farther. When eternity is finally done (if such a thing can be contemplated), God's mercy will still endure. It never runs out, is never exhausted; and when you feel you have used up your allotment of mercy, you discover that there is an infinite river flowing from God's throne.

God's mercy is not like the weather. It does not change with the seasons, and it does not depend on you or on anything you may do. There is nothing you can do to make God love you more, and there is nothing you can do to make him love you less. His mercy is so great and his love so free that it is truly infinite and everlasting. *We see God's love and mercy most clearly at the cross.* While walking by a bookstore one day, I saw a plaque that read, "I asked Jesus, 'How much do you love me?' 'This much,' he answered. And he stretched out his arms and died." Fix your eyes upon the bloody cross of Calvary. Gaze upon the dying form of the Son of God. There you will find grace unmeasured, mercy undeserved, and love beyond degree.

No changes, however great, can produce any changes in him. *All things are moving according to God's divine plan.* There are no mistakes with the Lord. You may think it otherwise, but it is not true. You may say, "All things are against me," but it is not so. All things are for you, but you may not yet see it. God is ordering all for the best.

God and My Great-Grandchildren

Consider the final phrase in Psalm 100: "through all generations" (v. 5). It literally means "from generation to generation." Exodus 20:6 tells us that God shows his love to "a thousand [generations]" of those who love him. Since a biblical generation is 40 years, this means God's love lasts at least 40,000 years. And since this promise was given to Moses at Mt. Sinai approximately 3,500 years ago, we may safely conclude that God's faithful love will continue at least another 36,500 years. That is to say, in 3,500 years we are not yet even 10 percent of the way through the length of God's love. But surely that is not literal, you say. Indeed, it is not. But it is not purely figurative either. It's a way of showing us that God's love and faithfulness go far beyond any human understanding. Suppose we line up a grandfather, a father, a son, a grandson, and a great-grandson on a platform. This text tells us that

- what God is to the grandfather, he will be to the father;
- what God is to the father, he will be to the son;
- what God is to the son, he will be to the grandson;

- what God is to the grandson, he will be to the great-grandson.

And so it goes across the centuries. Generations come and go, one after the other. Only God remains forever.

I am so glad that God's faithfulness transcends the generations. I am fifty years old heading for . . . what? Fifty-five? Sixty? Seventy-five? Maybe eighty or even ninety years old if God blesses me with long life. But I won't live forever. As the years roll by, I find myself realizing how much of my life is wrapped up in my three boys. Yesterday they were in grade school, today they are almost grown up, and tomorrow they will be grandfathers. Will God still take care of them? What about their children? And their grandchildren? Will God still be there for them? *The answer is yes* because God's faithfulness doesn't depend on me but on the character of God, which spans the generations. That means I don't have to stay alive to ensure that my boys will be OK. God will see to that. After I am gone from this earth, and even if all my prayers have not been answered, I can trust God to take care of my boys. What a comfort this is. I can do my best to help my boys while I'm here, and after I'm gone God's faithfulness will continue for them and for their grandchildren, and even for their great-grandchildren.

Since God's faithfulness spans the generations, we can trust that his promises will still be good a thousand years from now. In that spirit, stop right now and pray for the next four generations—your children, grandchildren, great-grandchildren, great-great-grandchildren—born and yet-to-be-born.

"But I lavish my love on those who love me and obey my commands, even for a thousand generations." (Exodus 20:6, NLT)

The Real "Happy Hour"

God's faithfulness is our hope at the edge of death. This is why we rejoice as we bury our dead. Nothing of God dies when a man or woman of God dies. We need not fear death because a Christian is immortal until his work on earth is done. You cannot die and you will not die until God's appointed time. Until then, you are immortal. I do not know how far we have to go until we reach the end of our earthly road, but this I know—that road is paved with God's love and faithfulness. And we need not be afraid.

Lloyd Ogilvie, retired chaplain of the United States Senate, notes that Psalm 100 "makes a strong case for gladness as the sure sign that we are living by grace and not our efforts."[1] What a striking thought that is. *Happy Christians honor God.* There are places where you go to have "Happy Hour." But why should Christians need alcohol to be happy or joyful or filled with praise? Spurgeon commented that "our happy God deserves to be worshiped by a happy people." He's right. If our hearts are not filled with joy as we contemplate the Lord, if we are so uptight that no one would ever associate the word "gladness" with us, perhaps we need to discover the grace of God all over again.

A Prayer to Keep You out of Trouble

During an interview with Jerry Rose on the Total Living Network, he mentioned that many years ago an older man who had built a large and successful ministry offered him an important piece of advice. The man said there was a prayer he should pray every day because it would keep him out of trouble. Jerry went on to say that he had tried to pray that prayer every day since then, and he had found that the man's advice was true. What was the prayer? The older man advised Jerry to pray the last sentence of the Lord's Prayer every day: "Yours is the kingdom, yours is the power, yours is the glory, forever. Amen" (see Matt. 6:13). That's a part of the Lord's Prayer that most of us don't even think about, but it is absolutely crucial. We pray "Yours is the kingdom" because we know that the kingdoms of the earth will give way to the kingdom of the Lord Jesus Christ. We pray "Yours is the power" because we do not give up in the face of difficult trials but instead live in faith that the Lord has a purpose and will give us whatever we need to face the challenges of each day. We pray "Yours is the glory" because we have chosen to live for God instead of for the praise of men. We need to pray this way because we are all kingdom builders who love to operate in our own power and for our own glory. Therefore we must continually say to the Lord, "Not my kingdom but yours, Lord. Not my power but yours, Lord. Not my glory but yours, Lord. And not just today or tomorrow but forever. Amen." If we pray like that, and if we live like that, we'll stay out of the kind of trouble that could destroy us.

Three Simple Statements

As we wrap up this chapter, let me boil the application down to three simple statements:

1. God Owns Everything; We Own Nothing

Our problem is that too often we don't feel our need until things aren't going well. But we need God just as much when we have a million dollars as when we are flat broke. We need him just as much when our health is good as when we have cancer.

We need the Lord. We need him desperately. We need him more than we know.

2. Our Lives Are Broken because of Sin

Sin has messed up everything. The whole world groans and travails because of sin. Nothing works right, things break, little children are shot by the side of the road, marriages disintegrate, promises are broken, laws are violated, and terrorists fly airplanes into buildings. The world is broken, and we are broken. Like Humpty Dumpty, nothing we do can put us back together again.

3. If God Doesn't Help Us, We're Sunk

Our desperate need for God should be pretty obvious by now. I love how David puts it in Psalm 34:6: "This poor man called, and the LORD heard him; he saved him out of all his troubles." Take that verse backward and you come to a wonderful truth: If you want to be saved, the Lord must hear you. But to be heard, you must call on the Lord. Yet only a "poor man" calls on the Lord. Those who think themselves self-sufficient have no need for God, so they never call on him. *Only the "poor man" calls, and only he is heard, and only he is saved and delivered.* Is not this what Jesus meant when he said, "Blessed are the poor in spirit, for theirs is the kingdom of heaven" (Matt. 5:3)? Blessed are the poor in spirit, and those who mourn, and the meek who confess their weakness. They will enter the kingdom of heaven, they will be comforted, and they will one day inherit the earth.

Blessed are the needy . . .
Blessed are the desperate . . .
Blessed are the broken . . .
Blessed are the weak . . .

They will find the Lord! Everyone else will be turned away. It is only to the needy that God says, "Come on in. I have a place reserved for you."

Get off Your High Horse

If you ever travel to the Holy Land, you will visit the Church of the Nativity in Bethlehem. The church is built over the reputed spot where Mary gave birth to Jesus. To get to the church, you first walk across a broad plaza and then come to a very small entrance. In fact, it's so small that you have to duck down low to get inside. The entrance is deliberately made low because several centuries ago the local rulers liked to ride their horses into the sanctuary. The priests felt that was inappropriate, so they lowered the entrance to force the great men to dismount before entering the church.

The same is true of salvation. *If you want to go to heaven, you've got to get off your high horse.* Until you do, you'll never be saved. Since you don't deserve heaven, the only proper response to God's offer of salvation is to say, "Thank you, Lord God, for what Jesus did for me." Gratitude, not arrogance, is the language of heaven.

Jesus Is All You Need

If the First Law of the Spiritual Life drives us to our knees, the Second Law keeps us there until we cry out for mercy. It is a great advance in the spiritual life to bow before the Lord and say, "Oh God, I need you. I can't do this myself. Please help me." No one who has cried out to the Lord like that has ever been turned away. When we finally get off our high horse and cry out to God, then (and only then) are our prayers finally heard and answered. *But you'll never know until you see for yourself.* Your pastor can preach all day long, but it will have no effect until you admit how much you need the Lord.

Some of us have to hit rock bottom before we will finally look up and cry out to God in desperation. Years ago I heard it said this way: *You'll never know if Jesus is all you need until Jesus is all you have. When Jesus is all you have, then you will know that Jesus is all you need.*

Jesus said, "Apart from me you can do nothing" (John 15:5). Take a moment to pray about that statement.

- Tell the Lord how much you need him.
- Thank him for his mercy to you.
- Tell God you want to depend wholly on his strength today.
- List several specific areas in which you need his help.
- Agree with God that you will do his will wherever he leads you.

If you find it difficult to pray like this, ask the Lord to make you willing to be willing to surrender yourself completely to his moment-by-moment control.

Church of the Pathetic Losers

Several years ago during the annual pastors conference at Moody Bible Institute, Alistair Begg, pastor of Parkside Church in the

Cleveland area, spoke on our need to depend fully on the Lord and not on our own resources. As he came to the close of his talk, he told the story of how King Jehoshaphat prayed in 2 Chronicles 20. The Ammonites and the Moabites had been moving in a vast army toward Jerusalem. There were so many of them, and they were so well armed, that the men of Israel would never be able to defeat them. As the invaders came closer and closer, the situation looked increasingly hopeless. The king called for a nationwide fast. Men from every town and village gathered in Jerusalem to seek the Lord.

King Jehoshaphat stood before the people and offered one of the greatest prayers in the Bible (see 2 Chron. 20:6–12). First, he declared God's greatness: "O LORD, God of our fathers, are you not the God who is in heaven? You rule over all the kingdoms of the nations. Power and might are in your hand, and no one can withstand you" (v. 6). He reminded God of the promises he made to take care of his people when they were in trouble. Then he told God that they were in big trouble now: "We have no power to face this vast army that is attacking us" (v. 12). He concluded with this simple confession: "We do not know what to do, but our eyes are upon you" (v. 12).

God's answer came through a prophet. He told the people to *"stand still and see the salvation of the LORD"* (v. 17, NKJV). The next day Jehoshaphat put the male singers at the head of the army and sent them out to do battle. They literally stood still and watched as the Lord sent confusion into the enemy ranks. The Moabites and Ammonites started killing each other by mistake. There was a great slaughter followed by the plundering of the supplies left behind by the enemy soldiers. The story ends with the army gathering for a praise celebration, giving thanks to God for the victory he provided.

After telling that story, Alistair Begg commented that when Jehoshaphat prayed, "We do not know what to do, but our eyes are upon you," he was really saying, "Lord, we're just a bunch of pathetic losers. And if you don't help us, we're sunk." He went on to say that he had discovered that this was the true mission statement of the church he pastors: "We're just a bunch of pathetic losers and if God doesn't help us, we're sunk." That's a good name for a church: The Church of the Pathetic Losers. You would never run out of prospective members.

Blunder Forward

I think Alistair Begg is absolutely right. Apart from God's grace, that's all we are—just a bunch of pathetic losers. Without God we don't have a chance, we don't have a thing to offer, and we don't even know what to do next. Sometimes I think the hardest job God has is getting his children to admit how desperately they need him. So let me say it clearly to everyone who reads these words: *I am a pathetic loser.* Apart from the grace of God, I own up to the truth that in me—that is in my flesh—there is nothing good at all. Whatever talent I possess and whatever good I have accomplished, the power to do it has come from the Lord, and he alone gets the credit.

At the same pastors conference, Dr. Joseph Stowell, president of Moody Bible Institute, commented that many days he is just sick of himself. I understand that statement and say "Amen" to it. When I mentioned that to my own congregation, a man told me he had stayed up all night wrestling with the Lord because he too was sick of himself. A woman added, "Sometimes I get on my own nerves." And a man struggling with a cocaine addiction came to me asking for prayer that he might have the courage to share his struggles with his Sunday school class. Later I received E-mails from people who were touched by the same truth. All of us (if we are honest) are sick of ourselves sooner or later.

I heard of a pastor who came up with a phrase that he printed at the top of their church bulletins even though some of the leaders didn't feel comfortable with it: "Blunder Forward." Having been a pastor for more than a quarter of a century, I can testify how true that is. Even on our best days, we struggle as God's people to simply "blunder forward." And some days we can't even do that. One of our church's missionaries responded to my "pathetic losers" comment this way: "All of us know that it is the absolute truth, so why deny it? Why not get it out in the open and deal with it? Why is it so hard for us, and especially us evangelicals, and *especially evangelical leaders,* to be simple, transparent, humble, and open? Why is it so hard to get *down* (yes, I said 'down') to where God is? He is humbler than we are! He is 'lower' than we are!"

Jesus told us how to live when he declared, "For whoever wants to save his life will lose it, but whoever loses his life for me and for the gospel will save it" (Mark 8:35). In the kingdom of God, all the values of the world are reversed. The way up is down. The last shall be first. The least will be the greatest. The servants will be the leaders.

Are we really "pathetic losers"? Yes, and we don't know the half of it. Every day we should pray, "Lord, save me from myself."

We need to pray for each other. We need to pray for our spiritual leaders. Let's not put our leaders on such a high pedestal that we think they are beyond mistakes or not in need of our prayers. Apart from God's grace, *all* of our leaders are pathetic losers. There are no exceptions. It is when pathetic losers band together to seek the Lord that the Red Sea parts, the walls come tumbling down, the enemy is routed, and the church rolls on for the glory of God.

A TRUTH TO REMEMBER:

You'll never know if Jesus is all you need until Jesus is all you have. When Jesus is all you have, then you will know that Jesus is all you need.

God doesn't need us, but we desperately need him. This is the Second Law of the Spiritual Life.

GOING DEEPER

1. Read Ephesians 2:1–10. According to this passage, what is our true condition before coming to Christ for salvation? How did God reveal his love for us (vv. 4–6)? What does it mean to say that we are saved by grace through faith (see v. 8)? Why do many people have trouble accepting this truth?

2. Is it getting easier for you to say, "I was wrong"? Why is confession such a vital part of the spiritual life? What happens when we refuse to confess our sins? What sin do you need to confess right now?

3. Why do so many people have to hit bottom before they finally cry to God for his help?

4. Read Psalm 91 and underline all of God's promises to you. Write out a prayer thanking God for all the times he has

protected you, including those times when you were not aware of his protection.

5. "Apart from God's grace, we're all pathetic losers." Do you agree with that statement? Why or why not?

6. Psalm 100 instructs us to enter his courts with praise and to come into his presence with thanksgiving. Take three minutes to write down every reason you can think of to praise the Lord for his goodness to you. Then pick a hymn or a praise chorus and sing it to the Lord.

CHAPTER 3

The Third Law:
What God Demands,
He Supplies

*T*HE SEVEN LAWS OF THE SPIRITUAL LIFE cover the basic principles of the spiritual life that apply to all Christians everywhere. These are truths that every Christian needs to know because they meet us right where we are and then take us all the way home to heaven. The First Law states a fundamental reality: *He's God and We're Not.* Get this, and everything else in life will begin to fall into place. Skip this, and nothing will work right. If you are unclear about who's God and who's not, the rest of the spiritual laws won't help you a bit. But once you rip that "big G" off your sweatshirt, you are in a position to grow spiritually. As long as you fight with God, your frustrations will follow you no matter how often you go to church. It is a great advance in the spiritual life to finally say, "The battle is over, Lord. I'm putting down my weapons. You win." The First Law leads us to healthy submission, where we can say from the heart, "O God, not my will but yours be done."

The Second Law takes us one step further: *God Doesn't Need Us, but We Desperately Need Him.* The key is the word *desperately,* which focuses on our weakness, our sinfulness, and our total separation from God because of our sin. God can get along fine without us, but we couldn't live another second without him. Once we realize our true condition, we end up on our knees, confessing our sin and crying out to God for mercy.

And that leads us to the Third Law of the Spiritual Life: *What God Demands, He Supplies.* This is a wonderful word of hope for those who find themselves face down in the dust, with nowhere else to turn. The Third Law brings us to the very heart of the gospel. If we understand this law, we know why the gospel is truly Good News.

An Old Testament Illustration

Let's begin with a very familiar story from Genesis 22. One day God came to Abraham and told him to take his son Isaac to the region of Moriah and sacrifice him there as a burnt offering to the Lord. The words of Genesis 22:2 emphasize the close bond that existed between father and son: "Take your son, your only son, Isaac, whom you love." There are many questions we would like to ask at this point, foremost among them being, Why would God ask a father to sacrifice his own son? Isn't the very request a violation of God's nature? If there was any discussion between Abraham and God, or if Abraham hesitated when he heard the command, it is not recorded in the text. All we know is that the next morning Abraham took his son and his servants and set out to obey the Lord's command.

When they got to the region of Moriah (modern-day Jerusalem), Abraham said to his servants, "Stay here with the donkey while I and the boy go over there. We will worship and then we will come back to you" (Gen. 22:5). One wonders what he was thinking and how much he understood. Hebrews 11:19 indicates that he thought that God would raise his son from the dead. Somehow Abraham looked beyond the immediate circumstance and found faith to believe that the God who would take his son from him could also give him back.

As father and son walked along together, Isaac asked a question that must have torn at Abraham's heart. "Father, I see the wood and the fire, but where is the lamb for the sacrifice?" (see v. 7). With an even greater flash of insight, Abraham replied, "God himself will provide the lamb for the burnt offering, my son" (v. 8). Across the centuries Christians have seen in these words a prefiguring of the death of Christ on the cross. There is Abraham (representing God) placing Isaac (representing the Jesus Christ) on the wood (representing the cross). It is the father offering his son freely and without complaint, just as God the Father offered Jesus for the sins of the whole world. Somehow Abraham understood something of the doctrine of substitutionary atonement. When he said, "God himself will provide the lamb," he was pointing not simply toward the altar on Mount Moriah, but to a greater sacrifice to be offered at the very same location almost two thousand years later when God provided the ultimate Lamb—Jesus Christ—for the sins of the world.

When they reached the right spot, Abraham built an altar of stones and placed the wood on top of it. Then he bound Isaac and placed him on the wood. I don't know what words passed

---

If God ever asked you to do something like he asked Abraham to do, how do you think you would respond?

_____

_____

_____

---

between father and son, but I doubt that much was said. What does a father say to his son in a moment like that? What does a son who loves and trusts his father say as his hands and feet are bound? Then came the moment of truth. Abraham raised his hand and prepared to plunge the knife into the breast of his son. At that very instant, not one second sooner and not one second later, God spoke to Abraham: "Do not lay a hand on the boy . . . Do not do anything to him. Now I know that you fear God, because you have not withheld from me your son, your only son" (v. 12). Again, the timing was crucial. As Abraham looked up, he saw a ram caught by its horns in a nearby thicket. I am sure he ran to get that ram before it freed itself and got away. With the same knife that he would have used to take his son's life, he slit the ram's throat, drained the blood, set the wood on fire, and offered the ram on the altar to the Lord.

Only one detail remained. Abraham called the place "The LORD will provide" (v. 14). The traditional English rendering of the Hebrew is *Jehovah Jireh*. The word *jireh* comes from a Hebrew word meaning "to see" or "to provide." Abraham meant, "Here is the place where God saw my need and provided the ram to meet my need."

In a broader perspective, we can sum up the whole story in three short phrases:

God saw.

God demanded.

God provided.

He saw everything, he demanded a sacrifice, and he provided what he demanded. As we read this story, it's easy to focus on Abraham's amazing faith. But the real hero of the story isn't Abraham. *The real hero is God!* As great as Abraham was, God was even greater. He gave Abraham a seemingly impossible demand and then he provided what Abraham lacked—a morally righteous way to meet the demand. God did what only God could do. He supplied what Abraham needed to fulfill his demand. What God wanted all along was not the death of Abraham's son but rather Abraham's unquestioning obedience. He never meant for Isaac to die, but it had to happen the way it did in order for Abraham to demonstrate his faith and for God to demonstrate his grace.

Blood, Death, Sacrifice

The story of Abraham and Isaac happened early in the history of the Old Testament. Several hundred years passed. One day God spoke to Moses on Mount Sinai and gave him the law that would guide the people of Israel. If you have read Leviticus, you know that God gave Moses instructions regarding various offerings and sacrifices. From our point of view, it was a fairly complex system that involved offering different animals to be sacrificed before the Lord. It might be a lamb or a goat or a bull. In certain cases it could be a turtledove. The priest would take the animal, kill it, drain the blood, and burn the carcass on the altar of sacrifice. And the law was very specific. The animals had to be unblemished. No broken bones. No sores. No disease. No animals with one eye. No crippled animals. They must be "without spot or blemish." All other animals were turned away.

Even a casual reading of Leviticus reveals that the Old Testament religious system was very bloody. If you were a priest, you spent a good part of every day killing animals, draining their blood, in some cases splashing the blood on the altar, in some cases preserving part of the animal for food, and then burning the rest on the altar. All day long that was your job. Killing, draining the blood, burning the carcass. Day after day, week after week, month after month, year after year. No matter how hard you tried to wash it off, you would go home with the smell of blood and burning flesh on your clothes.

Blood

Death

Sacrifice

That was the religion of the Old Testament. If you served as a priest for forty years, you would have killed thousands and thousands of animals. The blood would have filled a small lake. And when you died, another priest would come along and take your place and do the same thing. Blood, death, sacrifice. There was no end to the killing, no end to the bloodshed, no end to the death because that's the religion God gave to his people. Hebrews 10:11 summarizes the entire religious system of Judaism in a few succinct words: "Day after day every priest stands and performs his religious duties; again and again he offers the same sacrifices, which can never take away sins." The whole routine of priests in the Old Testament involved an intricate system of sacrifices and offerings—one after the other, morning, noon and night, day in and day out, week in and week out, month in and month out, year after year, decade after decade, century after century. During the 1,500 years from the time of Moses to the time of Christ, hundreds of thousands of lambs and goats and bulls were offered on the altar before God to make atonement for the sins of the people. That's what the writer means when he says "day after day" and "again and again" the same sacrifices were offered.

And note that Hebrews 10:11 says that the priests were standing as they offered all those sacrifices and offerings. If you read Exodus and Leviticus, you will find a description of the architecture of the ancient tabernacle. Moses writes at great length concerning the coverings of the rings and of the poles. You will find a description of the brazen altar, of the shewbread, of the candlesticks, of the veil, and of the furniture that went inside the Holy of Holies—all described in minute detail. But there is one thing that you will not find described in the furniture of the tabernacle. You will never find a description of a chair—because there were no chairs in the tabernacle. That's because when the priests were standing before God to minister, they could never sit down. Why? Because they could never finish with the work of making sacrifices and offerings before God. The Greek word in Hebrews 10:11 for "take away" is really a word that means "to strip off," as if you were wearing tight-fitting clothing like a sports uniform. It pictures a uniform that is soaked in sweat so that you have to strip it off at the end of the day. It's a picture of the sin that entangles us and besets us and seems to wrap around us. The writer is telling us that though you offered a thousand goats and a thousand bulls and a thousand rams, all the blood of all those animals added together couldn't take away one sin. Not even one.

Do you really think that God enjoyed seeing animals killed? Do you think God was pleased with a river of animal blood? Do you think God enjoyed the smell of burning animal flesh? Micah 6:6–7 poses the question this way: "With what shall I come before the LORD and bow down before the exalted God? Shall I come before him with burnt offerings, with calves a year old? Will the LORD be pleased with thousands of rams, with ten thousand rivers of oil?" Hebrews 10:8 (quoting Ps. 40) answers very plainly: "'Sacrifices and offerings, burnt offerings and sin offerings you did not desire, nor were you pleased with them' (although the law required them to be made)." Whatever else one can say about the sacrificial system, *it was not God's ultimate desire.* From the very beginning, he always planned something better. Hebrews 10:1 tells us that the law was a "shadow" of good things to come. It was a divinely ordained object lesson, teaching the Israelites through the monotonous repetition of blood, death, and sacrifice that they dare not approach God on their own but only through the sacrifice of something (or Someone!) offered on their behalf.

No Unemployed Priests

The priest in the Old Testament had very steady employment because he was always offering sacrifices. He was so busy he could never sit down. Here's the kicker: he had a job that was guaranteed to bring him nothing but frustration, because every time he made a sacrifice, it never really took away sin. He had to make another one, and he had to make another one, and he had to make another one.

So his wife would say to him in the morning, "Honey, what are you going to do?" And he'd say, "Well, I'm going to go up to the tabernacle." She'd say, "What are you going to do when you get up there?" "We'll offer a lamb first." "What are you going to do after that?" "Well, I think I'm going to offer a couple of goats." "What about after that?" "Probably do the grain offering." "What do you think you'll do after that?" "When the High Priest comes in, we'll probably do a bull." "What about after that?" "Well, we'll probably have lunch." "What are you going to do after lunch?" "Probably do some more goats and maybe pray awhile and sing a few songs and along about sundown we'll do the evening sacrifices—do some lambs, another goat." "Will you be home in time for supper?" "Yes, I'll be home in time for supper." "What are you going to do tomorrow?" "The same thing I'm going to do today." That was the life of a priest in the Old Testament.

Guaranteed Frustration

It was the same old thing over and over and over again in accordance with the law of God. It wasn't that he had a bad job. Far from it. He was doing exactly what God prescribed, following the instructions in Exodus and Leviticus. It wasn't his fault. He was just following orders.

But even though the priests of the Old Testament did their job in accordance with what God had said, it was guaranteed to bring futility and frustration. They would come to the end of their lives, and as soon as they were buried, on that same day someone would be appointed to take their place because the sacrifices and offerings had to continue because it was impossible for the blood of bulls and goats to take away sin. What a futile job.

Let me put it another way. Suppose you were a priest in the Old Testament. Now, suppose that you lived not the normal fifty or sixty or seventy years, but you lived to be one thousand years old. From the day you were born to the day you died you offered a lamb in the morning and a lamb in the evening. You never missed a day, and you never missed a lamb. By the day you died you would have lived 365,000 days and you would have offered 730,000 lambs to God. Do you know how many sins you would have forgiven? Not one. Zero. No sins. That's not much to show for one thousand years of work. Ever, ever, ever working and never, never, never forgiving, not even one sin.

A Messy, Smelly Job

If you took all the bulls and all the goats and all the turtledoves and all the lambs and all the rams and all the other animals that were offered in sacrifice to God, and if you took them and looked at all those sacrifices made over a 1,500-year period, it would be a veritable river of blood. Though you had the river of animal blood before you, not one sin could it forgive. Not one. "Because it is impossible for the blood of bulls and goats to take away sins" (Heb. 10:4).

Can you imagine what kind of life it must have been for priests of the Old Testament? Killing animals for a living. Cutting the throat and spilling the blood and sprinkling it before God. Then taking part of the body and burning it before God every day. Burning one animal after another in an offering and sacrifice before God. Can you imagine what that was like?

Have you ever seen an animal sacrifice? Have you ever seen a goat slaughtered? I saw it when we were in Haiti on a missions trip. It happened about 11 o'clock in the morning. I was up in the orphanage where we were staying, and Nathan Burk was with me. I think I was drinking a Coke and making my notes on the Gospel of John. Suddenly we began to hear the bleating of a goat outside our window. It wasn't the normal sound a goat makes; it was a frightened bleating—faster and faster and louder and louder. It sounded like an animal in trouble. Nathan looked out the window and said, "They're going to kill that goat." I said, "No, they're not." He said, "Yes, they are."

I went and looked out, and sure enough, down by a cactus plant there were two teenage boys on top of the goat. One of them had a knife, and they were about to slaughter that goat. Nate and I being curious types, we walked outside and stood about six feet away. There was blood everywhere. Blood on the cactus. Blood on the goat. Blood on the knife. Blood on the ground. It was awful. To make matters worse, they couldn't get the goat killed. That was the horrible part. They had a knife, but it wasn't sharp enough. They had half the throat cut, but they couldn't get the goat killed. Eventually they had to go inside to get a butcher knife so they could finish the job. They made a big hole in the goat's throat, and the blood came pouring out. Meanwhile the goat was making a terrible racket. It was one of the most awful scenes I have ever witnessed. Finally they found the right thing to cut, and the animal went into convulsions and finally died.

Now that's what the priest did for a living. One after the other, a goat, a lamb, a ram, a bull. Every day he went to work and put those animals to death. Every night when he came home, the smell of death and blood was all over him. The next morning he had to get up and do it all over again because his work was never finished.

The New Testament Fulfillment

The entire legal system of the Old Testament was meant to prepare the Jews for the day when John the Baptist saw Jesus and exclaimed, "Look, the Lamb of God, who takes away the sin of the world!" (John 1:29). What an amazing statement that is. Why? Well, *first, Jesus is God's lamb sent from heaven to earth*. If *we* offer a sacrifice, the best we can do is to offer a literal lamb or a goat or to round up a bull and bring it to the priest. Animal blood was what we could offer. When *God* offers a "lamb," that "lamb" is his own Son. He is the perfect sacrifice. All those animals the priests put to death were meant to point directly to Jesus.

Second, Jesus is God's lamb offered for our sins. The word translated "takes away" is used elsewhere for the rolling away of the stone that sealed the tomb of Jesus. When our Lord died on the cross, he "rolled away" our sins once and for all. They are gone, removed, blotted out, covered, and rolled away forever.

Third, Jesus is God's lamb who rolls away the sins of the world. I was thinking about those Orthodox Jews who were murdered in Jerusalem by a suicide bomber. They were still looking for the Messiah; they didn't believe he came two thousand years ago. But

Jesus died for them too. And he even died for the bomber who took his own life while taking theirs. Here is an amazing truth: *The blood of Jesus is so powerful that it is sufficient payment for the sins of the whole world.* Anyone, anywhere, at any time can be forgiven through Christ. There are no barriers that stand between you and eternal life. Jesus paid it all.

Hebrews 10:12 explains it this way: "But when this priest had offered for all time one sacrifice for sins, he sat down at the right hand of God." The first word of that verse is the key. Take a look at the word *but.* Circle it. Underline it. Your salvation depends upon that one little word *but.* You are going to heaven because of that little word *but.*

On one side stand the priests doing the will of God day after day, week after week, and year after year—killing the animals, making the sacrifices, making the offerings before Almighty God. Their hands are stained with blood. The same thing every day, all the time. And when one of them dies, another one steps up to continue the offerings and sacrifices. Always standing, never sitting down because their work is never finished because the blood of bulls and goats can never take away sin.

On the other side stands one man. His name is Jesus Christ. And between the priests of the Old Testament and Jesus Christ there's the little word *but.* And that word makes all the difference. After they had done all the killing they could do, in accordance with the will of God and fulfilling the Old Testament Law, they could never take away sin. *But,* Jesus did what they could never do. He sat down—because his work was finished. One man, one offering, paid for sins forever. He finished it, and then he sat down at the right hand of God.

No Bull in Church Today

By any chance did you bring a goat to church last Sunday? Did anyone park a bull outside the church? Did any of you bring a turtledove? Do you know why you didn't? You didn't because in that little word *but* we don't have to do that anymore. Did you ever wonder why we don't sacrifice animals on Sunday morning? We don't need that anymore. "But when this priest had offered for all time one sacrifice"—not of a bull, not of a goat, not of a ram, not of a lamb—"when he had offered for all time one sacrifice"—of his own body on the cross—"for sin" (Heb. 10:12). Do you remember what he cried from the cross? "It is finished" (John 19:30). What he meant was the work of redemption was done. It is finished. The price has been paid. It is finished. The sacrificial system is finished. No more bulls. No more goats. No more lambs. It is finished and gone forever because when Jesus died it was one for all and once for all—always and forever complete. Finished and done. So he sat down. His work was done.

This is the difference between Christianity and all the other religions of the world. The other religions of the world are stand-up religions. They have to stand up and keep on working. They have to stand up and keep on giving. They have to stand up and keep on praying. They have to stand up and keep on sacrificing. They have to stand up and keep on obeying the man-made rules of a man-made religious leader. They're stand-up religions. But thank God, we don't have a stand-up religion. Because of Jesus Christ we have a sit-down salvation. If you want to go to heaven, you can try to go standing up or you can go sitting down. If you try to go standing up, you will never make it. You will never be good enough. You'll never sacrifice enough. You'll never be perfect enough. If you go sitting down, it's because you are trusting in what Jesus Christ did on the cross for you. That's what I mean by a sit-down salvation. Jesus did the standing so you could do the sitting.

Jesus Christ has accomplished in his death what the Old Testament priesthood could never accomplish. The priests were good men. Nothing that I've said should be made to appear as if they weren't good men or in the will of God, because they were. It was God's will that they offer those sacrifices. But Jesus Christ has done what they could never do. He has accomplished a sit-down salvation. Sometimes we say that practice makes perfect. That's true in sports. That's true in playing the piano. It's true of most things in life. But practice does not make perfect when it comes to the forgiveness of sins. You'll never get your sins forgiven just by practicing something over and over and over again—like coming to church, like saying a prayer, like being good, like keeping the Ten Commandments. When it comes to forgiveness, practice does not make perfect.

An Eternal Truth

All of this leaves us with a hugely important principle that I will state this way: There is something in God that causes him to provide whatever we need to meet his righteous demands. That "something" is his grace. The word means "unmerited favor" or "undeserved bounty" and refers to the fact that God's generosity moves him to give us what we do not deserve and could never earn. It literally means that he gives us the exact opposite of what we deserve—which is eternal punishment in hell.

Here is the whole gospel in three simple statements:

God said, "Do this."

We said, "We can't."

God said, "All right. I'll do it for you."

God demanded perfection. We couldn't meet the standard, so God sent his Son, who was perfect, in our place.

God demanded payment for sin. We couldn't make the payment, so God sent his Son, who paid the price in full on our behalf.

God demanded righteousness. All we had to offer were the filthy rags of our soiled self-righteousness, so God sent his Son, who took our sin so that we might be clothed with his perfect righteousness.

God demanded a scapegoat who would be rejected and sent away. When Christ died bearing our sins, the Father turned his back on his own beloved Son so that Jesus cried out, "My God, My God, why have you forsaken me?"

God demanded a bloody sacrifice for sin. We couldn't meet that demand, so he sent his Son to die in our place, shedding his blood, paying the price, bearing our burden, offering himself as the final sacrifice for our sin.

Blood. Death. Sacrifice. The Old Testament system made it clear that that is what God demands because of our sin. Without blood, without death, without sacrifice no one can come into God's presence. But we weren't even qualified to die for ourselves, much less for anyone else. We weren't perfect, or pure, or unblemished. Sin had marred every part of us, inside and out.

If God didn't do something for us, we were sunk.

His holiness demanded a perfect sacrifice.

His love sent us his Son.

In this we see the glory of the gospel. God said, "You must." We said, "We can't." God said, "I will." And he sent his Son from heaven to earth to do for us what we could never do for ourselves. The Bible repeatedly declares that salvation comes from the Lord (Exod. 15:2; Jonah 2:9; Pss. 37:39; 62:1; Isa. 45:17; Acts 4:12). Everything starts with God. Salvation doesn't start on earth and rise to heaven. No, a thousand times no. It starts in heaven and comes down to earth. God takes the initiative. He makes the first move. That is why the most famous verse in the Bible begins this way: "For God so loved the world that he gave . . ." (John 3:16). You'll never understand why Jesus came until you grasp the meaning of those words. Jesus is God's gift to the human race. Entirely undeserved. A gift given in spite of our sin. A gift many would despise and reject. A gift that would be brutally crucified. But even his crucifixion was part of the gift from God, for in his death he gave us eternal life.

We can expand this thought in many directions:

- God knew we were dead in our sins, so he sent Christ to give us life.
- He knew we were his enemies, so he sent Christ to make us his friends.
- He knew we were like orphans, so he sent Christ to bring us into his family.
- He knew we had no hope, so he sent Christ to give us a home in heaven.
- He knew we were poor, so he sent Christ to make us rich.
- He knew we were enslaved, so he sent Christ to set us free.

- He knew we were afraid to die, so he sent Christ to die and then raised him from the dead.
- He knew we had nothing, so he gave us all things in Christ.

What he demanded from us, he gave to us.

What we needed, he provided.

And there is much more:

- He knew we needed guidance, so he gave us his Word, the Bible.
- He knew we needed power, so he sent us the Holy Spirit.
- He knew we needed encouragement, so he gave us brothers and sisters in the church.

And he placed us "in Christ." At this point the great words of the gospel come into play: salvation, forgiveness, grace, mercy, love, peace, hope, eternal life, redemption, substitution, propitiation, reconciliation, adoption, justification, regeneration, and glorification. All of it is given to us freely in Christ.

Or think of the little word *new.*

New life

New hope

New heart

New mind

New standing

New position

New name

New power

New direction

New destiny

All of it is ours, all of it is free, and all of it comes to us as a gift from God through Jesus Christ our Lord. We didn't deserve any of it. We could never have earned it in a million years. Isaac Watts said it well in these words written nearly three hundred years ago:

Not all the blood of beasts
On Jewish altars slain
Could give the guilty conscience peace
Or wash away the stain.
But Christ, the heav'nly Lamb,
Takes all our sins away;
A sacrifice of nobler name
And richer blood than they.

Who Is a God Like You?

Once we finally begin to understand what God has done for us, we quite naturally ask: "Who is a God like you, who pardons sin and forgives the transgression of the remnant of his inheritance? You do not stay angry forever but delight to show mercy" (Mic. 7:18).

Who is a God like you? Where else will we find a God like this? He is a God who delights to show mercy to sinners like you and me. He loves to forgive sin. He longs for sinners to come to him. He sends his Son to die on the cross and then says to the whole world, "Anyone who wishes may take the free gift of salvation."

There is no other religion in the whole world like Christianity. We are the only people in the world who preach free grace. Ours is the only free religion in the world. Every other religion says, "Do this and live." Our God says, "It has been done for you." And right there you find the whole gospel in just three little words:

Do vs. Done

Every other religion is based on works. You go to heaven because of what you do: Give money. Go to church or to the synagogue or the mosque. Pray toward Mecca. Light a candle. Pray all night. Keep the feast days. Give alms to the poor. Offer a sacrifice. Keep the Ten Commandments. Be baptized. Follow the Golden Rule. Be a good neighbor. Don't get in trouble. Obey the law. Stay out of jail. Be courteous, kind, and forgiving. Try harder. Do your best. Follow the program. Live a good life. In looking at that list, it's important to note that many of those things are indeed good and right and noble, but the problem with a religion based on "doing" is that you can never be sure you've done enough. And if somehow you finally do enough, how do you know that you won't blow it all tomorrow by one stupid sin?

But Christianity is based on grace. Sometimes you hear the phrase "free grace," but that is a redundant statement. If it's not free, it's not grace. If you have to do something, anything at all, to earn it or merit it or deserve it, it's not grace. Grace is no longer grace if you have to do something to earn it. The whole difference comes down to this: Christianity is based on what Christ has done for us. Every other religion is based on what we ourselves do.

Do this and live, the law demands,
But gives me neither feet nor hands.
A better word the gospel brings,
Bids me fly and gives me wings.

Christianity vs. Radical Islam

Let me make the point a bit sharper. In recent months world attention has been focused on the radical version of Islam that causes young men to hijack planes and blow themselves up in the service of Allah. We can summarize the difference between radical Islam and biblical Christianity this way:

In radical Islam God tells you to send your son to die for him.

In Christianity God sends his Son to die for you.

Who wouldn't serve a God like this?

Let me bring the discussion to a very fine point. Are you satisfied with what Jesus did for you on the cross? If you are, then all you have to do is rest on him for your eternal salvation. If you aren't satisfied with what Jesus did, then you've got to do something to add to his work on the cross.

God is satisfied with what Jesus did.

Jesus himself said, "It is finished."

The price has been paid in full.

What do you say? Is Jesus enough to take you to heaven, or do you think you've got to add to what he did?

Let me explain what all this means. *Because of the work of Christ on our behalf, we now have full forgiveness for all our sins.* Not only that, we have the assurance that when we die, we will go to heaven. We can even say with confidence that the worst sinner can be saved—anytime, anywhere. The door to heaven has been opened by the bloody death of God's Son. Will you not go through the door marked "Enter by Grace"?

Which of the following statements best expresses your understanding of why Jesus had to die?

_____He died as a martyr because he was a threat to the powers-that-be.

_____He died as a good example to show us how to love others.

_____He died in order to unite all people into a religion of peace and world harmony.

_____He died because he was a sinner just like anyone else.

_____He died in our place, taking our sin upon himself, bearing the punishment for our sins so that we might be forgiven and have eternal life.

"We all, like sheep, have gone astray, each of us has turned to his own way; and the LORD has laid on him the iniquity of us all."
(Isaiah 53:6)

Craig Kozlowski

A few months ago I was the speaker for a breakfast sponsored by the men's ministry of Moody Church in Chicago. When I arrived at the restaurant at 7:30 A.M., I put on my nametag and walked into the room. About forty men had gathered for the meeting. As I looked around, I realized I didn't see anyone I knew. Then a man walked up to greet me. He was about my size and height, and his face seemed vaguely familiar. I noticed that he was walking with a cane, which I presumed was from some sort of injury, probably while playing sports. When I looked at his nametag, I knew who he was. Craig Kozlowski and his wife, Marion, had attended Calvary (the church I currently pastor) in the early 1990s for about a year or so. Later they moved to the far western suburbs, and a few years ago they moved to downtown Chicago, which is when they started attending Moody Church. I hadn't seen Craig for several years, but I remembered his story.

He came to Calvary because Marion talked him into it. She had been raised by missionary parents, had drifted from the Lord, and upon recommitting her life to Christ, had started attending Calvary. In early July 1991 she finally talked Craig into coming with her. That Sunday I was preaching on the words of Christ from the cross: "It is finished" (John 19:30). I explained that the phrase comes from the Greek word *tetelestai,* which means "paid in full." When Christ died in our place, he fully paid the price for our sin so that there is nothing else that needs to be done and nothing we can do to add to the value of his death on our behalf. *Because Christ paid our debt, we are saved simply by trusting in his work on our behalf.* Although Craig had gone to church for many years, he had never heard that message before. That day changed his life forever. He trusted Christ as his Lord and Saviour. A year or so later I got a letter from him telling me that he had purchased a boat and named it *Tetelestai.* He even sent me a picture of the boat with the name in big letters on the back. Whenever people asked about the strange name, he shared his testimony with them. Craig reminded me when I saw him that it was the sermon on "It is finished" that God used to bring him to Christ.

So I asked him why he was walking with a cane. "I've got terminal cancer," he replied. A few months previous the doctors had discovered an aggressive form of prostate cancer that had spread to his spine and was moving throughout his body. He was only fifty-one years old. He said matter-of-factly, "I've got less than a year."

A Win-Win Situation

You can learn a lot from a man who knows he is about to die. Craig told me that when he heard the news, at that very moment the peace of God flooded his soul and he knew he would be all right no matter what happened. "Are you afraid to die?" I asked. "No, I'm not afraid to die. I know where I'm going." He said it with the calm assurance of a man who knows the Lord. Later he added, "This is a win-win situation for me. I get to enjoy my family and my friends for a few more months, and then I get to see Jesus in person. I spend a lot of time now thinking what that will be like. I can't imagine how wonderful heaven will be." When Erwin Lutzer, pastor of Moody Church, joined us at the table, he looked at Craig and said, "This man proves the gospel is true." Craig heard the message, he believed in Jesus, and now he's not afraid to die.

That's the difference Jesus makes. God's timing is always perfect. While I was finishing this manuscript, I received a call saying Craig had just died. When I spoke with Marion, she told me that during his last few months Craig mentioned he hoped the Lord would give him a tiny glimpse of heaven in advance. The day before he died, she heard Craig mumble the word "heaven." Later he told his daughter the Lord had given him the glimpse he hoped for. Now he has seen it for himself. Now he has seen Jesus face-to-face.

Truth in Action

As we wrap up this chapter, let me share two simple applications:

A. If God has provided all that we need, then we must reach out and receive what he offers.

> Nothing in my hand I bring,
> Simply to thy cross I cling.

Jesus himself made the invitation very clear when he said, "Come to me, all you who are weary and burdened, and I will give you rest" (Matt. 11:28). The psalmist encourages us to "taste and see that the LORD is good" (Ps. 34:8). And the words of Isaiah 1:18 offer this hope to seeking hearts: "'Come now, let us reason together,' says the LORD. 'Though your sins are like scarlet, they shall be as white as snow; though they are red as crimson, they shall be like wool.'"

Come to me . . . taste and see . . . let us reason together. How simple it is to be saved. Just reach out your empty hands and take the gift God offers you.

B. If we have experienced God's free grace, we ought to respond with profound gratitude.

God has done it all. He has made a way for lost sinners to be forgiven. He found us, saved us, redeemed us, gave us new life, and set us on the road to heaven. Should we not give thanks to our great God every single day? If the truth of grace does not move your heart, either you don't understand your sin or you don't understand what God has done for you. We come to Christ by faith, and the rest of our life is one big P.S. where we say "Thank-You" to the Lord.

Properly understood, the Third Law has an important corollary:

What God demands, he provides.

What we receive, we give away.

Consider the words of Jesus in Matthew 10:8, "Freely you have received, freely give." The whole gospel is contained in the first phrase; our entire response (to God and to others) is in the second. Salvation is free; we receive it as a gift; we freely give what we have received to others. The key word is *freely*. It means "without a cost," gratis, no charge, a gift with no strings attached.

Were you forgiven? Then forgive others.

Did God show mercy to you? Then show mercy to others.

Did the Good News come to you? Then make sure you pass it along to someone else.

Ponder this for a moment and you see how huge it really is. This is the whole foundation for the Christian ethic of love. This is the basis for Christian giving. This is the foundation for showing kindness to the poor. This is why we share Christ with others. This is the reason we send missionaries to the ends of the earth.

And from this principle comes a whole galaxy of spiritual disciplines:

- Gratitude
- Praise
- Worship
- Obedience
- Sacrifice
- Submission
- Cross-bearing
- Service

And from this rich fountain flows a river of countercultural values:

- Caring for the needy
- Visiting the prisoners
- Praying for our enemies
- Taking up our cross

- Rejoicing in tribulation
- Turning the other cheek
- Going the second mile
- Reaching across racial and ethnic barriers
- Standing up for what is right
- Becoming martyrs for Christ
- Forgiving others "seventy times seven" (Matt. 18:22)
- Asking forgiveness when we have hurt others
- Rejecting the ways of the world
- Giving beyond our means
- Giving thanks "in all things"
- Keeping our marriage vows
- Saying no to persistent temptation
- Serving Christ in a "forgotten" place
- Yielding our right to get even
- Loving those who don't love us
- Trusting God with our entire future

What God gives us, we return to him in praise, worship, service in the local church, daily obedience, submission in our trials, and perseverance to the end. C. S. Lewis illustrated this truth by imagining that a little child asks his father to give him sixpence so he could buy his father a birthday present. The father is pleased to give his child the money, and he is even more pleased to receive the gift. But it is not as if the father has been made richer by the gift, because he provided the money to buy the gift in the first place. He is "sixpence none the richer" (a contemporary Christian rock group took its name from this story). Lewis points out that we cannot give God anything that he does not already possess. He gave us everything, including life itself.

Anything we do for him is only returning to him what he provided to us in the first place.[1]

What God gives us, we pass along to others through intercessory prayer, daily obedience, acts of kindness, sacrificial giving, bold witness, missionary vision, and through a lifestyle of justice, humility, and mercy. Most of us have probably heard it said that evangelism is one beggar telling another beggar where to find the bread. Evangelism is more than that, but it's not less than that. When we share Christ, we are simply passing along to others what God has given us in Christ.

If we have truly been forgiven by God, what should our response be toward those who offend us? Are you up to date on your forgiving, or are you holding a grudge against someone who said or did something to hurt you?

_____

_____

_____

_____

"Be kind and compassionate to one another, forgiving each other, just as in Christ God forgave you." (Ephesians 4:32)

Robert Robinson wrote the hymn "Come, Thou Fount of Every Blessing" in 1758:

Come, Thou Fount of every blessing,
Tune my heart to sing Thy grace;
Streams of mercy, never ceasing,
Call for songs of loudest praise.

Teach me some melodious sonnet,
Sung by flaming tongues above.
Praise the mount! I'm fixed upon it,
Mount of Thy redeeming love.

A TRUTH
TO REMEMBER:

There is something in
God that causes him
to provide whatever
we need to meet his
righteous demands.
That "something" is
his grace.

There is an important first step if you are to enter into the truth of the Third Law: *Lay hold of the riches that are yours in Christ Jesus.* Lay aside the rags of your own righteousness and receive the pure white robes of the righteousness of Christ. Hold out your hands, and he will fill them with every spiritual blessing. All that God has promised is yours for the asking. Would you like the water of life? Come and drink all you like. It's yours, and it's free, flowing from the throne of grace in heaven. Think of what is yours through Christ:

He forgives with no payment for us whatsoever.

He forgives all our sins once and for all.

He promises complete reconciliation with God.

He gives you assurance of your salvation.

He makes you his child and adopts you into his family.

He places you in Christ.

He gives you access to God twenty-four hours a day, seven days a week.

He gives you a new heart and a new life.

He gives you a home in heaven for all eternity.

He promises to raise you from the dead.

He promises that you will be like him and will reign with him in heaven.

All of this is yours in Christ. Christian, does this not lift your spirit? Does it not make you want to sing? Why aren't you on your feet right now, praising the Lord?

Remember this truth: What God demands, he supplies. All we need, we find in Christ. And what we receive, we give to others. This is the Third Law of the Spiritual Life.

GOING DEEPER

1. Why don't we bring animals to church today to offer as sacrifices? What does Hebrews 10:1–4 tell us about the sacrificial system of the Old Testament?

2. Why are so many people attracted to the idea that there is something they must do in order to earn salvation from God? Why is the concept of grace difficult for many to grasp?

3. What does the death of Christ mean to you personally? Do you see any connection between his death and your life?

4. What did Jesus mean when he cried out from the cross, "It is finished" (John 19:30)?

5. Read Hebrews 13:15–16 and make a short list of the sacrifices you can offer to God in gratitude for what Jesus has done for you.

6. Think of several friends and loved ones who need to know Christ. What is keeping them from salvation? Spend some time praying for each person by name. Ask God to open each heart so they can respond to the gospel with true saving faith.

CHAPTER 4

The Fourth Law:
What You Seek, You Find

Sometimes we have to hit bottom before we finally look up.

The letter came from a man in prison in Virginia. I do not know the man, have never met him, and know nothing about him other than what he writes.

I have been incarcerated for the past 23 years, 12 months, and 21 days. I have been in prison for a total of four times of about 29 years. I am 58 years old, have three children of 35, 34, and 32 years old. I am divorced and live here in Virginia.

Here is the reason for his letter:

I am writing you to let you know that I have received a rich blessing from reading your book What a Christian Believes. *I have since accepted Christ Jesus into my life and now enjoy spiritual freedom— freedom from sin, fear, and slavery. Until a person is willing to say, "I am a sinner in need of salvation," he cannot experience such freedom from guilt and condemnation as I have. I was hopelessly enslaved by sin before I read your book and accepted Jesus into my life.*

He closes the letter by asking that I pray for revival at the correctional center where he is serving time. I have no idea who found a copy of my book and gave it to this man in prison in Virginia. There is a connection that only God knows. But it illustrates a great truth. Prison bars won't stop the Holy Spirit. *Circumstances are no obstacle to God.* When we truly seek the Lord, even behind prison bars, we will find him.

Throughout this book we have been looking at the Seven Laws of the Spiritual Life. These "laws" are not exactly doctrines, not exactly duties, not exactly promises, and not exactly rules. Each one represents a major truth that Christians need to know. They are like pillars that hold up a large building. Here are the first three:

The First Law: He's God and we're not.

The Second Law: God doesn't need us, but we desperately need him.

The Third Law: What God demands, he supplies.

These three laws lay a theological foundation that prepares us for everything that follows. They lead us to three words of response: submitting, admitting, receiving. We submit because "he's God and we're not." We admit that "we desperately need him." And we gratefully receive what God supplies in order that his righteous demands might be fully met. *The Third Law summarizes the entire gospel.* We are so lost, so sinful, so desperate, that if God doesn't intervene, we're sunk. But he does. And he gives us whatever we need for salvation, freedom from guilt, forgiveness of our sins, abundant life on earth, and a home in heaven when we die. Since grace is a gift, our most basic response is to gladly receive the gift God offers us. And what we freely receive, we gladly give away.

Seeking and Finding

Now we're turning a corner in our journey. The Fourth Law takes us into the realm of practical Christian living. It tells us that "what you seek, you find." Those five simple words challenge us at the level of personal motivation. As I prepared this chapter, I was struck by how much the Bible has to say about seeking and finding, especially seeking and finding the Lord. Here are just a few examples:

- "But from there you will seek the LORD your God, and you will find Him if you seek Him with all your heart and with all your soul." (Deut. 4:29, NKJV)

- "As for you, my son Solomon, know the God of your father, and serve Him with a loyal heart and with a willing mind; for the LORD searches all hearts and understands all the intent of the thoughts. If you seek Him, He will be found by you; but if you forsake Him, He will cast you off forever." (1 Chron. 28:9, NKJV)

- "He sought God in the days of Zechariah, who had understanding in the visions of God; and as long as he sought the LORD, God made him prosper." (2 Chron. 26:5, NKJV)

- "When You said, 'Seek My face,' my heart said to You, 'Your face, LORD, I will seek.'" (Ps. 27:8, NKJV)

- "Seek the LORD while He may be found, call upon Him while He is near." (Isa. 55:6, NKJV)

- "You will seek Me and find Me, when you search for Me with all your heart." (Jer. 29:13, NKJV)

- "But seek first the kingdom of God and His righteousness, and all these things shall be added to you." (Matt. 6:33, NKJV)
- "So I say to you, ask, and it will be given to you; seek, and you will find; knock, and it will be opened to you. For everyone who asks receives, and he who seeks finds, and to him who knocks it will be opened." (Luke 11:9–10, NKJV)
- "But without faith it is impossible to please Him, for he who comes to God must believe that He is, and that He is a rewarder of those who diligently seek Him." (Heb. 11:6, NKJV)

And this list is just the tip of the iceberg. The whole concept of "seeking God" is an enormous biblical concept that touches our motivation, our priorities, how we spend our time, the goals we set in life, and our spiritual growth (or the lack thereof).

Do you desire to know God better? Take a moment to write a prayer to the Lord expressing your hunger for an intimate relationship with him.

_____

_____

_____

_____

"As the deer pants for streams of water, so my soul pants for you, O God." (Psalm 42:1)

Clarifying the Issue

I'd like to summarize what these verses are saying in several simple statements:

A. Everyone seeks something. By nature we are all seeking people. Some people seek money, others fame, others pleasure, others self-validation, others sexual fulfillment, and others worldly power. We may seek a husband or a wife, or we may seek children or a new job or a better education or a new home or new friends or a new church. The tragedy of our time is that so many people are wasting their lives chasing after three things that can never satisfy—money, sex, and power. We want money, so we sacrifice our families to get it. We want sex, so we sacrifice our morals to get it. We want power, so we sacrifice our friends to get it.

And when we finally get it, it doesn't satisfy.

Duane Thomas, star running back for the Dallas Cowboys in the 1970s, had it right. He kept hearing writers refer to the Super Bowl as the ultimate game, so he asked the obvious question: "If this is the ultimate game, why do they play it again next year?" That's the way things are in the world. You climb to the top of the heap only to discover that next year you've got to start all over again. Nothing in this life satisfies forever.

B. There is an easy test to find out what you truly seek in life. This test is absolutely foolproof. *You tell me how you spend your time and your money and I'll tell you what you are seeking.* You can *say* anything you like. You can even come to church and look very religious, but your time and your money don't lie. Time is life, and money is nothing but the time it takes to make the money. Show me your calendar and your checkbook, and I'll know the truth about your priorities.

I read about a man who looked at his life and concluded that he was just like the Professor on *Gilligan's Island*. "The Professor knew how to turn banana peels into diesel fuel and he could take algae and make chocolate fudge, but he never got around to fixing that hole in the boat so he could get off the island. Same as me. I spent my life learning to do amazing things that didn't matter, and I ignored the hole in my boat. And that's why I'm stuck where I am."[1]

C. *Whatever righteous thing you seek in the spiritual realm, you can have it, if you want it badly enough.* "Blessed are those who hunger and thirst for righteousness, for they will be filled" (Matt. 5:6). This is one of the most stupendous promises in the Word of God. If you are hungry and thirsty for the righteousness that God provides, you will be filled.

If you want righteousness, you can have it. Let me go out on a limb and make a bold statement. *Whatever righteous thing you desire in the spiritual realm, you can have if you want it badly enough.* I don't think we appreciate the importance of that truth. Most of us are about as close to God now as we want to be. We have about as much joy as we want, about as much peace as we want. Abraham Lincoln said, "Most people are about as happy as they want to be." Totally true. We are the way we are because that's the way we want to be. Either we're happy that way, or we've accepted that this is who we are and we're not going to change. For the most part, you are where you are right now because that's where you want to be. *If you were hungry for something better from God, you could have it.*

If you want it, you can have a close walk with God.

If you want it, you can have a better marriage.

96

If you want to, you can do God's will.

If you want to, you can witness for Christ.

If you want to, you can learn to pray.

If you want to, you can grow spiritually.

If you want to, you can walk in the Spirit.

If you want to, you can become a man of God or a woman of God.

If you want to, you can change deeply ingrained habits.

If you want to, you can break destructive patterns of behavior.

What we seek, we find. This is true in every area and realm of life. Unless we seek, we will not find. And what we seek, for good or for ill, we eventually find.

How would you rate your walk with the Lord right now? Dying, stagnant, struggling, erratic, stable, growing, vibrant? What specific aspect of Christian character would you most like to develop over the next three months? What's the first step you need to take?

_____

_____

_____

_____

"But grow in the grace and knowledge of our Lord and Savior Jesus Christ." (2 Peter 3:18)

Removing the Excuses

Our primary problem stems from the excuses we make. We don't change and we don't grow and we don't seek God and we stay the way we are because that's pretty much the way we want to be. We've learned to live with mediocrity, and either we think things will never change or we're happy the way we are.

I can think of three excuses that keep us trapped in that terrible condition. *The first is the excuse of self-pity.* This excuse causes us to focus so much on ourselves that we virtually become the center of the universe. We can't be blamed; it's not really our fault; people treat us rotten; life stinks; we deserve something better; our feelings matter more than the truth. The list goes on and on. Self-pity is extremely popular—and extremely dangerous. It's a seductive lie that allows us to escape personal responsibility by deflecting attention away from the real problem. A classic biblical example comes from Jonah 4, after Nineveh repented and escaped God's judgment. Jonah responded with anger, saying that he wished God would take his life away because he would rather be dead than see Nineveh spared. First he was angry about the city being spared, later he was angry when a scorching sun made him feel faint, then he became angry that the vine God sent withered and died. The prophet was so full of self-concern that it didn't matter in the least to him that an entire city had been spared by God. He could only think about himself, in the process revealing his total lack of love and his total absorption in himself.

A man I had never met sent me an E-mail and then came to see me. He had graduated from an evangelical seminary and had served for many years as a pastor. After a series of serious moral

WHAT YOU SEEK, YOU FIND

failures became known, he lost his job, his reputation, his ministry, and his means of supporting his family. He was now trying to put the pieces of his life back together. He told me he had joined a support group of men struggling with the same sort of moral failures he had experienced. "It's a rigorous group," he said. They have one rule: *No self-pity.* No whining or complaining or moaning about what happened or how hard life is or how bad you have it or how if your wife had treated you better, you wouldn't be in this mess. "I've discovered that self-pity is the enemy of spiritual growth," he told me. He's right. As long as we mope around feeling sorry for ourselves, we can't get better. We'll be stuck right where we are.

The second excuse that keeps us from changing is the "I'm trying" excuse. I recently dropped by an Oak Park business and chatted with the owner, who happens to be a good friend. He is a Christian who has seen his share of hard times and has learned a great deal from his experiences. When I mentioned that I had been on the road and told him my schedule, he said, "You've been busy." "Yes, but I'm trying to slow down," I replied. He looked at me and said, "No, you're not. You're just failing at slowing down." Talk about a punch in the gut. That got my attention. He told me that whenever we say "I'm trying," that's just an excuse for not doing what we say we want to do. We can excuse any sort of non-performance by saying, "I'm trying." After I preached this, a friend told me we all know that lying is wrong. "But do you know what an excuse is? It's just a protected lie." She's right.

In one of the *Star Wars* movies, Yoda tells Luke Skywalker to use his powers to do something that seemed impossible. "I'll try," said Luke Skywalker. "No!" said Yoda. "Do or do not. There is no try."

You're either drinking or you're not drinking.

You're either reading through the Bible or you're not.

You're either paying off your credit cards or you're not.

You're either passing geometry or you're not.

You're either losing weight or you're not.

You're either swearing or you're not.

You're either using drugs or you're not.

You're either being faithful or you're not.

You're either forgiving that person who hurt you or you're not.

You're either getting married or you're not.

Saying "I'm trying" is just a weak excuse to take the pressure off yourself. You get credit for doing something that you're not really doing. In the end, it's a way of deceiving yourself into thinking you've changed when nothing has changed.

A friend put it to me this way in an E-mail:

When you used the example of people who are "trying to" quit smoking . . . lose weight . . . work out . . . read God's Word, etc., and that there really are no excuses and no self-pity for me if I am willing to accept responsibility for my condition, I am reminded of a principle I learned early in my AA career. It was the answer to people (me and others) who said that they were "trying to quit drinking." We were told that: "Trying is lying." It is lying both to myself and to anyone else who heard it. Further, if I wanted to lie to myself, that was one thing, but I was told that I should really have the decency not to waste the time of the group with that.

That little bit of truth had no varnish on it. It was really tough talk to hear and I didn't like it when it was directed at me. But I learned that the real answer was to "admit I was powerless to change myself," but that God "could and would if He were sought." He would relieve me of my compulsion to drink, drug, or whatever and He did . . . just like that . . . in the blink of an eye.

The third excuse that keeps us at a standstill in our spiritual growth is simply saying "I'll never change" or "I can't change" or "I don't want to change." If that's your bottom line, then I really don't have anything else to say to you. Until you want to change, you are doomed to stay exactly the way you are right now.

Which of these three excuses causes you the most problems in your daily life?

_____ I deserve something better.
_____ I'm trying.
_____ I'll never change.

Tiny Steps toward the Light

Galatians 5:16 instructs us to "walk in the Spirit" (NKJV). The Greek word for *walk* is very ordinary. It means to walk from one place to another. It's in the present tense, which means "keep on walking." To *walk* means "to take a series of small steps in the same direction over a long period of time." Walking implies steady progress in one direction by means of deliberate choices over a long period of time. To walk in the Spirit means something like "let your conduct be directed by the Holy Spirit" or "make progress in your life by relying on the Holy Spirit." *It conveys the idea of allowing the Holy Spirit to guide every part of your life on a daily basis.*

Walking is slow compared to driving a car or flying in a plane. It's not flashy at all. And sometimes walking can be tedious, dull, drab, and downright boring. Yet if you've got to get from Point A to Point B, walking will get you there, eventually. All you have to do is just start walking and don't stop until you get there.

A few years ago a woman came to see me. Because I thought I knew her fairly well, what she said blew me away. She told me that she was in the grip of an addiction that was destroying her life. By her own admission, she was in deep trouble because of her own wrong choices. Before we talked, I had no idea she had any sort of problem at all. None of her friends knew about it either. Now she was far gone in the darkness of addiction, with feelings of guilt and in deep despair of ever getting better. After listening to her story, I told her that she didn't get where she was overnight. It took thousands of wrong choices over a long period of time to get where she was. I also told her that she wouldn't be set free overnight either. She would have to take thousands of tiny steps toward the light before she would be free of the darkness.

Then the Lord gave me a liberating insight to share with her. Every day we make thousands of decisions. Most of them seem tiny and inconsequential. Certainly most of them seem to have no moral component. They are just little decisions we have to make. Will I get out of bed? Will I take a shower? Will I eat breakfast? If so, what will I eat? Will I drive to work? If so, what will I listen to while I drive? If I take the train, what will I read on the way to the office? Who will I talk to today? How will I relate to my coworkers? Where will I eat lunch? What time will I leave work? What will I say to my spouse as soon as I walk in the door? Will I sit down, or will I go play with my children? And on and on it goes, all the way down to something like, "Will I tie my shoes and tuck in my shirt today?"

The crucial insight is this: *There is no such thing as a truly neutral decision.* Because every choice we make is intricately linked with every other choice that came before it and with every choice we will make later, all our "little" choices are not really little at all. *Every choice we make either takes us a step toward the light or a step toward the darkness.* Even the "meaningless" choices lead us in one way or the other. The fact that we can't always see the implications of a decision doesn't mean they aren't there.

I told the woman that in order to get out of the darkness, she must go home and start taking tiny steps toward the light. And I warned her that the next morning when she woke up, she would still be in the darkness, so any steps she took toward the light would be steps of faith taken in the darkness. And the next day after that she would still be in the darkness. And the day after that. But if she kept on taking little steps toward the light, in a few days or a few weeks or in a month or two, one day she would wake up and see little streaks of light on the horizon. And one day, sooner or later, if she kept on walking in the light, she would wake up and see her room filled with the blazing light of God's love shining around her.

A few months after our meeting she wrote me a wonderful note. She said that when she left my office, she was determined to take tiny steps toward the light even though it was very hard at first. For many days she seemed to be walking in the darkness. *But God is always faithful to his obedient children.* Slowly the light began to dawn, and one day she woke to find her whole life bathed in light. She had been set free. That was seven years ago, and she's been walking in the light ever since. Not long ago she wrote me a note:

> *I will always remember when I was at my lowest and you once again took the time to talk to me and encourage me. You told me each day to walk toward the light, and as long as I walked more toward the light and less toward the darkness, I would be doing OK. I followed what you said, and one day a few weeks later, I woke up and the room was filled with light, and I knew it was God telling me, "Well done." Now it is seven years for me and I know, [every day is] just one step at a time, walking toward the light.*

What you seek is what you find. When you seek the light of God with all your heart, that is exactly what you find. But first you have to stop feeling sorry for yourself, stop making excuses, stop "trying," and start taking little steps toward the light. Let me say it very clearly: Walking in the Spirit is not some mystical experience reserved for a few special Christians. *It's God's design for normal Christian living.* It's nothing more than choosing (by God's grace) to take tiny steps toward the light day after day after day. Those tiny steps do not remove the struggle, but they allow you to walk in the light even while you feel the pull to go in another direction. The pull of the darkness is always with us in one form or another. By the Spirit's power, we can choose to walk in the light every day.

A question for personal reflection: *In what area of my life do I most need to start taking "tiny steps toward the light"?* Spend time in prayer before you answer. Pray for God to take down the inner barriers that keep you from seeing the truth.

If you are willing to start taking those tiny steps toward the light, then write the words "By God's grace, I will" in the space below.

_____

_____

_____

_____

"When Jesus spoke again to the people, he said, 'I am the light of the world. Whoever follows me will never walk in darkness, but will have the light of life.'" (John 8:12)

Life Applications

Let's wrap up this chapter with a simple question of application: *Are you a God-seeking person?* How would you answer that? What evidence in your life points in a positive direction? It is not enough to be religious or simply busy going to church events. As good as that may be, it's not the same thing as seeking God with all your heart.

Ask for Feedback

Let me ask you to do something that might be a bit difficult. Go to someone who knows you well and ask this question: "Am I a God-seeking person? When you look at my life, do you see the qualities in me of a person who truly seeks God?" If you'd like a fascinating test, go to an unsaved friend or relative and ask them that question. You may be surprised at how readily they answer. Unsaved people may not understand the intricacies of our faith, but they know the difference between someone who seeks God and someone who doesn't. In some cases I think unbelievers can be less easily fooled than believers. Since they don't focus on the outward trappings as much as we might, they can spot a God-seeking heart, even if that's not what they would call it. People who don't know the Lord instinctively recognize a person who truly knows God and seeks him passionately. This is a question a Buddhist can answer, or a Hindu, or a Muslim, or a Jewish coworker, or someone who isn't religious at all. Go ahead. Ask them, "Am I a God-seeking person?" They will tell you the truth as they see it. Or ask your husband or your wife (if you dare!). You certainly can't fool them. Or ask your children. (After I shared this truth with my congregation, a woman wrote that she had asked her children, and they unanimously told her that she was indeed a God-seeker. That's a wonderful affirmation.)

A Place to Begin

What should we do with the truth we have learned? If you want a God-seeking heart, where should you begin? I have five suggestions: *First, admit your need.* You cannot change until you admit that you need to change. If you are happy the way you are, then I have nothing to say to you. But if you are tired of turning banana peels into diesel fuel while there's a hole in your boat, then pay attention, because your life could be radically changed.

Second, cry out to God for help. I met a man who said, "It happened sixteen years ago today." What happened? "Sixteen years ago my life hit rock bottom. Alcohol had destroyed me. My marriage was gone, my career was ruined, and my life was a wreck. I had tried everything the world had to offer, and nothing seemed to make a difference. When I finally had nowhere else to turn, I cried out to Jesus. Sixteen years ago he heard my cry and changed my life." This man is living proof of the life-changing power of Jesus Christ. He cried out, and the Lord heard him and saved him from the pit of destruction. If you need the Lord, cry out to him today. Seek him with all your heart, and you will find him.

Third, surround yourself with God-seeking people. You know who they are. God-seekers aren't hard to spot. Find some friends who truly seek the Lord, and glue yourself to them. Go where they go; do what they do. Follow their example. Eventually one of two things will happen. Either they will drive you nuts and you will leave them, or they will rub off on you and you will become a God-seeker too.

Fourth, wait on the Lord. This is a hard discipline for most of us to practice. Our message to God is: "Give me patience, and give it to me right now!" We want spiritual maturity, and we want it by 11:30 A.M. We're not accustomed to waiting patiently on the Lord. But waiting has many positive benefits. The very act of waiting purifies our hearts and increases our longing to know the Lord intimately. As we wait and as we pray, we become like the deer panting for water. Our souls grow hungry to know the Lord.

Fifth, spend time in fasting. I believe there is a direct connection between biblical fasting and seeking the Lord. For some, that might mean going without a meal once a week in order to wait on God. For others, it might mean going a day without a meal. The ancient discipline of biblical fasting can be practiced many different ways. I have found it beneficial to take a day a week and fast from sunrise to sundown. And on occasion I have fasted for several days at a time. Fasting slows us down, reorients our perspective, weans us away from our love of the world, and puts us in a spiritual position where we can seek God with fewer distractions.[2]

The great mystic Thomas a Kempis (who wrote *The Imitation of Christ*) said, "Seek God, not happiness." Most of us have it all backward. *We seek happiness and hope to have God thrown in as a bonus.* But we end up with neither. The paradox of the gospel is that when we truly seek God, we find him, and we get happiness (deep fulfillment, lasting joy, the abundant life) too. But it takes years for many of us to figure that out, and some of us never get it straight. To the very end, we pursue earthly happiness and our own agendas, and wonder why life leaves us frustrated and disillusioned.

"Come unto Me"

I close with this final thought. *Jesus' appeal is always personal.* He never says, "Come and join the church," or "Come and be baptized," or "Come and give money." He simply says, "Come unto me." When Jesus says, "You will be filled," he means, "You will be filled with Jesus himself!"

If you are hungry, come and eat of the Bread of Life.

If you are thirsty, come and drink of the Water of Life.

If you are weary, come and find rest.

If you are guilty, come and be forgiven.

If you are far from God, come back home again.

The French philosopher Pascal said that there is a "God-shaped vacuum" inside every human heart. Since nature abhors a vacuum, if we don't fill it with God, we will fill it with something else. So many of us have filled our hearts with the junk food of the world. No wonder we are so unhappy. No wonder we jump from one job to another and from one relationship to another. We're like little children who won't let go of the marble in order to receive a diamond. "No, I won't give up my weekend affair for eternal joy." "Trade a broken marriage and a failed career for peace and forgiveness? Forget it." "Give up my drug addiction and be forgiven for all my sins? No way, man." "You say I can replace my anger and bitterness with peace and contentment? I can't take the chance. Sorry."

A TRUTH TO REMEMBER:
When we truly seek God, we find him; and we find true happiness as well.

No wonder we stay the way we are. We're trapped in the pit of a thousand excuses. We'd rather have misery and pain than risk it all on Jesus. Many centuries ago, Augustine explained both the problem and the solution: "O God, you have made us for yourself, and our hearts are restless until they find rest in you." *We will never be happy until we put God first in our lives.* And we can never do that until we surrender our lives to Jesus Christ once and for all.

Let me give you some good news. *In the kingdom of God, everything begins with a seeking heart!* Salvation begins with a hungry heart. If you are tired of the life you've been living, you can make a new start.

In the spiritual realm, what you seek is what you find. This is the Fourth Law of the Spiritual Life.

GOING DEEPER

1. What are the greatest desires of your heart? Do you believe it is God's will that those desires be fulfilled?

2. Read Jeremiah 29:13. List various ways in which people "search" for God. Why must the search be wholehearted in order to be truly successful?

3. Consider this statement: "Whatever righteous thing you desire in the spiritual realm, you can have if you want it badly enough." Do you agree? How should we define the phrase "righteous thing"?

4. Why is it dangerous to say "I'm trying" when we speak of some important goal we wish to accomplish? How can that become an excuse to cover our disobedience and inaction? Are you guilty of "trying" when you really ought to be "doing" in some area of your life?

5. Which of the five steps mentioned in "A Place to Begin" seem most important to you personally?

6. "There is no such thing as a truly neutral decision." Why is that statement so crucial when considered in the context of seeking freedom from debilitating habits and sinful patterns?

CHAPTER 5

The Fifth Law:
Active Faith Releases
God's Power

COURAGE is contagious.

A letter arrived from an organization called World Relief asking for prayer for the church in southern Sudan, site of ongoing persecution of Christians by radical Muslims. The facts were grim: churches looted, Christian villages burned, the wholesale murder of Christian leaders, and even stories about Christian children being sold into slavery. This is all accompanied by famine and widespread civil war. I knew a bit about this, and so I read the letter with interest.

Not long after that I was in Chicago taping an interview at the Total Living Network. Since they usually do a whole week in one day, guests from several programs meet in the "Green Room" before the taping. When I walked in, I spotted a nice-looking gentleman and his adult son. He immediately stood and said, "Hi, I'm Clyde Calver with World Relief." I recognized his name and mentioned that I had read his letter. It turns out that he had just returned from Sudan and was going to talk about it on the television program. When I asked if the reports about widespread persecution were true, he replied in the affirmative. Then he added a detail I hadn't heard. He said that in many places the church in southern Sudan is growing rapidly. Despite the persecution (or perhaps because of it), one church leader told him, "We've got too many converts. We can't take care of them all." That's a nice problem to have, isn't it?

How has it happened? An early church father named Tertullian gave the answer when he declared that the blood of the martyrs is the seed of the church. *You can kill the messenger but you can't kill the message.* For two thousand years, enemies of the gospel have done their best to wipe out Christianity. They may stop it in one place, but it springs up in another. Then when they turn around, it springs back up where they thought they had stamped it out. Too often we say, "I'm waiting for better circumstances." God says, "Go ahead and speak up. I don't need good circumstances in order to do my work." Hard times often give us fantastic opportunities to share the gospel with others.

A Quick Review

Let's begin by reviewing the first four laws of the spiritual life:

Law 1: He's God and we're not.

Law 2: God doesn't need us, but we desperately need him.

Law 3: What God demands, he supplies.

Law 4: What you seek, you find.

Each law covers a major area of our relationship with God and leads us to a personal response. Once we know that God is

God and we are not, we submit ourselves to his authority. This principle leads us to worship and praise. When we realize how desperately we need God, our logical response is to confess our sins and cry out to God for his mercy. This law introduces us to such concepts as human sinfulness, humility, and the importance of prayer. The good news of the gospel comes in the Third Law. Here we reach out with the empty hands of faith to receive what God offers us. This principle teaches us about God's love, compassion, mercy, and grace, and leads us to gratitude, joy, and the deep confidence that God will give us whatever we need whenever we need it. It provides us with hope in hard times and calls us to respond with praise and a life of glad obedience to God, who has lavished us with the riches of his grace. The Fourth Law brings us into the realm of spiritual motivation. It washes away our flimsy excuses and challenges us to seek God's kingdom above everything else. Here we encounter the power of the Holy Spirit and the importance of our daily choices.

The Fifth Law—Active faith releases God's power—moves us into a new area. Faith is the most prominent word in religion. Sometimes the word refers to an entire religious system, such as Christianity or Islam or Judaism. In other contexts it refers to a body of doctrine, such as, "Keep the faith." But most of the time faith refers to our personal response to God. The "faith" of the Fifth Law is not a religion or a set of doctrines, but rather our daily, moment-by-moment trust in God. When our faith is put to work, when it is active and not passive, it releases God's power in us and through us.[1]

We know from Hebrews 11:6 that *without faith it is impossible to please God.* No matter how religious you may be, if you do not have faith, you cannot please God. This may come as a surprise to those who have trusted in their religiosity to get them to heaven. But God looks on the heart, and what he looks for is faith. You can be baptized, go to church, give money, attend Sunday school, read your Bible, fast three times a week, sing in the choir, and even be a missionary; but if you do not have faith, you will not please God. Faith, genuine faith that comes from the heart, matters more to him than anything we say or do.

Everything by Faith

Faith is never meant to be a one-time experience. In evangelical circles, it is tempting to fall into that way of thinking because we put so much emphasis on being saved by faith. We talk about accepting Christ, receiving Christ, trusting Christ, and giving our hearts to Christ. We challenge people to respond in faith to the gospel invitation. This is well and good, but sometimes we leave the impression that once we have been saved by faith, the rest of life is up to us. Not so! *The same faith that saves us is the faith that carries us from day to day as we make the journey from earth to heaven.* That's why the Bible says, "The righteous will live by faith," and we are told that the gospel reveals a righteousness that is "by faith from first to last" (Rom. 1:17). *The whole Christian life is a life of faith.* We are saved by faith, kept by faith, walk by faith, endure by faith, rejoice by faith, serve by faith, love by faith, sacrifice by faith, pray by faith, worship by faith, and obey by faith. We get married by faith, and we have children by faith. (When I commented to my congregation that we get married by faith and have children by faith, there was a hearty "Amen!" from the audience.) All that we do, we do by faith.

The question before us in this chapter is both simple and profound: *What is faith, and how does it work?* This is a crucial topic because I think we often don't appreciate how precious and how precarious is the life of faith.

Faith Defined

In the entire Bible there is no clearer instruction on faith than Hebrews 11. Most of us know it as the "Hall of Fame of Faith." Here we have a long list of Old Testament heroes, most of them introduced with the phrase "by faith."

By faith Abel (v. 4)

By faith Enoch (v. 5)

By faith Noah (v. 7)

By faith Abraham (v. 8)

By faith Isaac (v. 20)

By faith Jacob (v. 21)

By faith Joseph (v. 22)

By faith Moses' parents (v. 23)

By faith Moses (v. 24)

By faith the people (v. 29)

By faith the walls of Jericho fell (v. 30)

By faith Rahab the prostitute (v. 31)

And the writer didn't even have time to mention the individual exploits of "Gideon, Barak, Samson, Jephthah, David, Samuel and the prophets" (Heb. 11:32). They and all the other heroes of the faith are summarized in this fashion: "Who through faith conquered kingdoms, administered justice, and gained what was promised; who shut the mouths of lions, quenched the fury of the flames, and escaped the edge of the sword; whose weakness was turned to strength; and who became powerful in battle and routed foreign armies. Women received back their dead, raised to life again" (vv. 11:33–35a). That's a wonderful list, and we can all think of the great biblical heroes who did these things.

But that is only part of the story. Verses 35b–38 record the trials of faith: "Others were tortured and refused to be released, so that they might gain a better resurrection. Some faced jeers and flogging, while still others were chained and put in prison. They were stoned; they were sawed in two; they were put to death by the sword. They went about in sheepskins and goatskins, destitute, persecuted and mistreated—the world was not worthy of them. They wandered in deserts and mountains, and in caves and holes in the ground." Who were these poor, benighted souls? What had they done to deserve such punishment? The writer simply called them "others." *They are "others" who lived by faith.* These men and women who endured such torment were living by faith just as much as Noah, Abraham, Moses, or Joshua. Their faith was not weaker. If anything, their faith was stronger because it enabled them to endure incredible suffering. They are not "lesser" saints because they found no miracle. If anything, they are "greater" saints because they were faithful even when things didn't work out right.

Moving against the Tide

Hebrews 11:39 gives us a summary statement of the whole list: "These were all commended for their faith." As we stand back and study this list, three factors quickly emerge. *First*, though these individuals are widely separated by time and space (and by personality and individual achievement), they are joined by one common factor: What they did, they did by faith. This is why they won God's approval. There isn't much that joins Abraham and Rahab except that at a crucial moment in life, they each acted in faith. God saw their faith and rewarded it.

Second, living by faith often meant moving against the prevailing tide of public opinion. Noah built an ark; Abraham left Ur; Moses rejected Egypt; and Joshua marched around Jericho. The same principle holds true today. If you decide to live by faith, you will definitely stand out from the crowd, and you may face opposition and ridicule.

Third, Hebrews 11 demonstrates that the life of faith is not a rarity. It's easy to look at Enoch or Noah or Joseph or Moses or David and say, "I could never do that." Down deep in our hearts, we have believed a lie that the life of faith is restricted to a few "special" people. We think we could never qualify to have our names added to the list of Hebrews 11. But that's the very reason this chapter is in the Bible, so that we would know that these are ordinary men and women who did extraordinary things simply because they had faith in God. They are made of the same stuff as we. The life of faith is within the reach of every believer. If we desire it, we can live like this too.

Hebrews 11:1 offers us a concise definition of faith: "Now faith is being sure of what we hope for and certain of what we do not see." I personally prefer the traditional King James rendering of this verse because it is more picturesque: "Now faith is the substance of things hoped for, the evidence of things not seen."

The word *substance* is an unusual word that refers to the "essential nature" of things. It was sometimes used to refer to the foundation of a house, and outside the New Testament it was used for the title deed to a piece of property. Faith is the "title deed" to things in the future, things hoped for, things promised by the Lord. *It is confident assurance that what we hope for will someday come to pass.* The word *evidence* refers to legal proof in a courtroom. Faith is proof to the soul that enables us to see things that cannot be seen by the naked eye. By faith we "see" what would otherwise be invisible.

Holy Discontent

There is a sense in which living by faith requires a measure of holy discontent. *You've got to want some things that you don't have in order to have faith because faith always deals with things "hoped for."* If you've already got everything you need and want and desire, and if for you all the promises of God have already come true, and if you've reached a state of spiritual perfection, if all your prayers have been answered, and if all your loved ones are saved and serving the Lord, if there is no lack anywhere in any area that you can see, you don't need faith because you're living in heaven already and you just don't realize it. If you are satisfied with the current state of affairs, then you can skip this chapter altogether because it doesn't apply to you.

One Sunday I was late entering the second worship service because of something that happened while I was walking through the basement corridor to enter the sanctuary. A man in tears stopped me and asked if I could talk to him. I didn't have any time right then, so I asked if I could pray with him. Through his tears he said that he had spoken with his son the night before and had learned some heartbreaking news. The details were both personal and tragic, and I didn't have any easy answers for him. We prayed, and I left to enter the service. Later I reflected that as long as we live in a world where fathers get bad news from their sons, we will need faith. As long as marriages break up, and children suffer, and as long as the killing continues, and our leaders disappoint us, and as long as there is hatred and violence and prejudice and all manner of evil in the world, we will need faith because the "things hoped for" have not yet come to pass.

If you could ask the Lord Jesus for one thing for your church, what would it be?

_____

_____

_____

_____

As you seek to live by faith . . .
- say a prayer for the leaders of your church.
- name several areas where you can see God at work right now.
- pray for a spirit of love, unity, and a deep commitment to God's truth.
- pray for openness to the Holy Spirit's leading.
- ask the Lord to use you as an encourager to others in the congregation.
- pray that unbelievers will see God at work in the church.

"Now to Him who is able to do exceedingly abundantly above all that we ask or think, according to the power that works in us, to Him be glory in the church by Christ Jesus to all generations, forever and ever. Amen." (Ephesians 3:20–21, NKJV)

What, then, is faith? Think about the following three words: Believe. See. Do.

Faith believes *what others do not believe.*

Faith sees *what others do not see.*

Faith does *what others do not do.*

True faith is never passive. True faith moves us to act, to do, to try, to build, to attempt, to expand, to say no to sin and yes to righteousness, to join, to speak out, to move forward, to dare to dream beyond our means, and to walk around Jericho again and again until at last "the walls come tumblin' down." A man in my Promise Keepers group offered this definition: *Faith is "outrageous trust" in God.* I like that. "Outrageous trust" is what you have when you build an ark hundreds of miles from any body of water. "Outrageous trust" compels you to leave your home not knowing where you are going. And "outrageous trust" sends you into the Elah Valley to face Goliath. Have you ever been in a situation where you needed "outrageous trust" in God? If not, I think your Christian life has been too boring!

Faith Illustrated

Let's pause for a moment and take a closer look at the case of Moses. The heart of his story is found in Hebrews 11:24–27.

By faith Moses, when he had grown up, refused to be known as the son of Pharaoh's daughter. He chose to be mistreated along with the people of God rather than to enjoy the pleasures of sin for a short time. He regarded disgrace for the sake of Christ as of greater value than the treasures of Egypt, because he was looking ahead to his reward. By faith he left Egypt, not fearing the king's anger; he persevered because he saw him who is invisible.

Note the five words that tell his story: *refused . . . chose . . . regarded . . . persevered . . . saw.* He said no to one thing because he chose to do something else. He made that choice because he regarded God's promises as true. He found the strength to endure forty years in Midian because he "saw him who is invisible." Everything hinges on the first word: He *refused* to be called the son of Pharaoh's daughter. That may not seem like much to us, but it was a life-changing decision for him. Recall that when Pharaoh's daughter found him floating in a basket near the shore of the Nile River, she rescued him and raised him as her own son. That meant he received a complete Egyptian education in science, history, and philosophy. It meant he was trained to be a leader of the nation. It meant he was raised in the lap of luxury, having the best of everything at his fingertips. Some scholars suggest that in those days the line of succession passed through the daughter of Pharaoh. If so, that means Moses was in line to become the leader of the most powerful nation on earth. The upshot is this: *Moses had everything he wanted and everything that most people would give anything to have.* He had power. Clap his hands and in came a dozen men to do his bidding. Clap again and servants delivered trays of food. Whatever he wanted, he could have.

A Different Path

Here is the irony of it all: When Moses got to the height of his power, *he gave it all up.* Refused it. Relinquished it. Let it all go. It was not an easy decision to make because he knew that no one, least of all Pharaoh's daughter, the woman to whom he owed his life, would understand. It seemed foolish, as if he were throwing away his whole future. By any normal standard, it didn't make sense.

"If they suffer, I will suffer."

Note how the text puts it: "He chose to be mistreated along with the people of God." It doesn't call them "the Jews" or "the Hebrews," even though those terms would be accurate. Moses didn't make his decision on a racial or ethnic basis. It's as if Moses stood in front of the Egyptians and said something like this:

You thought you knew me, but you didn't. I'm not one of you, and I've never been one of you. I may look like you and talk like you and dress like you and act like you, but down deep in my heart, I'm a different person. All these years in your midst haven't changed my basic identity. Those Hebrew slaves who seem so troublesome to you, I'm one of them because they are the followers of the true and living God. Though you hate and despise them, they are my people and I cannot stand by and turn my face away while they are suffering. If they are hated, I will be hated too. If they suffer, I will suffer. If they are mistreated, then I will be mistreated with them. What happens to them will happen to me. I will no longer live as if I were an Egyptian because I'm not. I am a follower of the God of Abraham, Isaac, and Jacob, and it's time I cast my lot with my own people.

And with that one act, Moses committed what we might call today "career suicide." He gave up the riches of Egypt and the "pleasures of sin for a season" (v. 25, KJV) in order to join the motley band of Hebrews who were so hated by the Egyptians. He found the strength to endure the persecution because "he saw him who is invisible." Now think about that statement. *It is one of the most remarkable and revealing statements in the entire Bible.* It appears to be an impossibility. How do you "see" an invisible person? The whole point of being invisible is so that no one can see you. If you can be seen, you are not invisible. But God was invisible, yet Moses "saw" him. How? Two words: "by faith." *Moses had faith, and his faith gave him sight.* He saw the God who is invisible.

The Egyptians didn't see. But Moses did. That's what faith can do.

How should you respond to a call from God when you don't feel adequate to the task and when you know that many people will not understand your decision?

_____

_____

_____

_____

"The one who calls you is faithful and he will do it."
(1 Thessalonians 5:24)

Seeing Beyond This World

What exactly did Moses see? The text says he was *"looking ahead to his reward."* Let me explain it this way. Moses knew that there were two worlds and that he could choose to live by the values of either one. There was the world he could see—the world of Egypt; the world of the senses; the world of money, power, sex, pleasure, fame, self-gratification; the world of military power and brute force. That was the world where Pharaoh ruled as king. As far as the Egyptians knew, that was the only world there was. The "gods" they worshiped were nothing more than an extension of their own perverted values. But there was (and is) another world. The invisible world of the spirit—the realm of God, the Lord Jesus Christ, the angels, and the saints. It's a world that is ruled by righteousness and entered by grace.

Now here's the kicker: *Those who live for this world will have the reward this world offers.* They will live for forty, fifty, sixty, seventy, eighty, or maybe even ninety years, and they will have as much fame or wealth or power as they can amass. Their reward from this world will be in this world. And when they die, all that they lived for will die with them. They will be buried in a box in the ground and have nothing substantial to show for their time on planet Earth. *But* (and this "but" makes all the difference) *those who live in this world by the standards of the eternal world have an entirely different experience.* Like Moses, they may suffer in the short run, but when they die, the party will just be getting started. They will enter into "the joy of the Lord." And frankly, those who live in this world by the values of the next one will have deeper joy and greater satisfaction here—even while they are being rejected and ridiculed by those around them.

Somehow Moses saw all of this. He figured out that it wasn't worth it to live for Egypt. The "pleasures of sin for a season" didn't measure up against the joy of serving the Lord, even if that meant temporary suffering and putting up with a bunch of crabby Jews for forty years in the wilderness. It just didn't matter. For him, there was only one choice. He would suffer with the people of God. Period. End of discussion. If the people of Egypt didn't like it, or if they didn't understand it, so be it. He might have been Pharaoh if he had stayed, but that didn't bother him in the least. If he had stayed in Egypt, we would never have heard of him and I would be preaching about someone else today.

So the question is, In which world do you want to make your mark? If you want to make it big in Egypt, good luck. Have at it. You will have your reward, and you won't be happy when you get it. If you want to live for the next world, you can, but it will cost you something in the meantime.

Mozart's Head or a Dancing Girl

Let's return to the statement that Moses "saw him who is invisible." *Faith sees what is really there even though others see nothing at all.* Faith believes what is true even though others don't believe it at all. By faith we see reality, which means we see beyond the world around us. But that concept should not seem strange at all. After all, one of the most beloved hymns in the world ("Amazing Grace") contains this line: "I once was lost but now am found, was blind but now I see."

By faith we see what others do not see. Have you ever looked at one of those 3-D pictures that contain hidden images? When you first look at the picture, all you see are wavy lines or dots or perhaps marbles or stars or pieces of fruit. But if you look at the picture up close, and if you throw your eyes out of focus and turn your head a bit cockeyed, suddenly out jumps Mozart's head or a dancing girl or a giant bird. Since I have less-than-perfect eyesight, I have trouble with 3-D pictures. Usually the only thing I can see is a bunch of lines or something that looks vaguely like a head of cabbage. To my consternation, my wife, Marlene, can almost always see the "hidden" image. But just because I can't see it doesn't mean it isn't there. The "hidden" image is there whether I see it or not. It's the same way with the life of faith. *The "hidden world" of eternal reality is there whether we see it or not.* By faith we "see" it, even though the people of the world do not.

A friend sent me this definition: "Faith sees the invisible, believes the incredible, and receives the impossible." That seems to fit Moses' experience very well. It all starts with seeing the invisible. If we can do that, we will be able to believe the incredible, and—in God's time—we will receive the impossible.

Faith, mighty faith, the promise sees,
And looks to God alone.
Laughs at impossibilities,
And cries, "It shall be done."

Describe a time when you experienced God's provision in an unlikely way:

_____

_____

_____

_____

"Ask and it will be given to you; seek and you will find; knock and the door will be opened to you." (Matthew 7:7)

Faith Applied

As we come to the end of our study of the life of faith, we can draw three important conclusions about the nature of faith.

A. Faith is not a feeling but a conscious choice to believe what God has said.

We will never progress in the spiritual life as long as we stay on the plane of our feelings. If Noah had waited until he "felt like" building an ark, he might never have laid the first piece of gopher wood. And if Joshua had waited to "feel like" marching around Jericho, those walls might still be standing. *Feelings are important, but they are not the basis of true faith.* When you are in a hospital waiting room while a loved one is in surgery, you may or may not feel positive. In that moment, you must consciously choose to believe that God is who he said he is and that he will do what he said he would do. You'll probably have to make that choice a hundred times a day. Faith chooses, then acts, and the feelings follow.

B. Faith acts even in the face of doubt and opposition.

If we wait until all the circumstances are in our favor, we'll probably wait forever. David didn't wait for Goliath to go blind: he trusted God and walked down into the valley to face the giant. If we wait for our doubts to disappear, we'll have to wait a long time. Here's a simple definition of faith. It is "belief plus unbelief and acting on the belief part." Sooner or later, we all have to "act on the belief part." Abraham did. Moses did. Samuel did. All the heroes of the Bible "acted on the belief part." You can too.

But what if you face that proverbial "leap of faith"? What then? The following quote from Barbara Winter cheered me up when I ran across it this week: "When you come to the end of everything you know, and are faced with the darkness of the unknown, faith is knowing one of two things will happen. Either there will be something solid for you to stand on, or you will be taught how to fly."[2]

C. Faith sees what others do not see.

As I worked on this chapter, I kept thinking about my friends Mike and Betsi Calhoun. Mike is the director of the Bible club ministry for Word of Life. A few months ago we ate lunch together when I taught for a week at Word of Life Bible Institute in Pottersville, New York. Two months after that, their daughter Misty died in a huge pileup of cars on Interstate 75 near Ringgold, Georgia. Misty was only twenty-four years old, recently married, and had moved with her husband Bryan to Chattanooga, Tennessee. They had been very active in the ministry of Calvary Chapel in Chattanooga. Speaking of Misty's faith, Betsi commented that her daughter had lived so much for eternity that it wasn't surprising that she slipped away so early to live there forever. Several days after the wreck, the *Atlanta Constitution* carried an article that contained this quote from Mike Calhoun: "We are not blind." He went on to say that although Misty is gone, they know she is in heaven and that they will see her again.

"We are not blind." We know what has happened.

"We are not blind." We know where she is.

"We are not blind." We know we will see her again.

Is this just wishful thinking? Is it just the broken heart of a father speaking about his daughter? Oh no, a thousand times no. My friend Mike Calhoun has discovered what Moses found thousands of years ago. We are not blind; our eyes have been opened; we see what has happened; and we see beyond it to the eternal realities that cannot be taken away. *The pain of death cannot cancel the promises of God.* Mike and Betsi have seen "him who is invisible," and they know the truth.

Believing in Advance

My favorite definition of faith comes from Philip Yancey, who said, "Faith means believing in advance what will only make sense in reverse."[3] So many things in this life make no sense to us. I imagine that every person reading this chapter has a few very deep and personal questions that defy all human answers. We want to know why things happen the way they do and why couldn't things have happened some other way. It would be wrong to say that faith provides all the answers. It doesn't. Perhaps in heaven we will fully understand, or in heaven our desire to know will be transformed by our vision of the Lord. By faith we see things that are invisible to others, and by faith we believe in advance those things that right now make no sense but one day will make perfect sense because we will view them in reverse.

The world says, "Seeing is believing." God says, "Believing is seeing." We believe, therefore we see.

When You Need to Know, You'll Know

I saw the above principle in action several years ago when a young couple, recently graduated from Moody Bible Institute, came to see me. They had just finished the first part of a training course with a missions organization in the Chicago area. Their advisor told them they needed to talk with their pastor before making the next step, so they came to see me with the good news that God was calling them to the mission field. "Where do you want to go?" I asked. "We don't know," the husband replied. I looked at the wife, and she smiled in agreement. "You mean you have no idea at all?" "No idea at all." Then I held up my hand and moved it as if I were twirling a globe. "You mean that in all the world, you don't have even a tiny idea where you would like to go?" "No." I sat there silently for a moment, pondering the situation. No one had ever said anything like that to me before. Suddenly I had a flash of inspiration. Looking right at that young couple, I said, "I've got the answer. The reason you don't know is because you don't need to know because if you needed to know, you would know, but since you don't know, you must not need to know, because if you had needed to know by now, you would know by now, but since you don't know, you must not need to know because when you need to know, you'll know. If God is God, that must be true." They were dazzled and speechless, and I was pretty amazed myself because all of that just came popping out at the spur of the moment. We prayed, and they left my office, still smiling.

Not long after that, I happened to meet a young lady from our church who works at Moody Bible Institute. Her job in the music library was scheduled to come to an end in a few months. Our paths crossed in the sanctuary lobby between services. When I asked her what she planned to do next, she said she had no idea. On the spur of the moment I decided to try it again:

"The reason you don't know is because you don't need to know because if you needed to know, you would know, but since you don't know, you must not need to know, because if you had needed to know by now, you would know by now, but since you don't know, you must not need to know because when you need to know, you'll know. If God is God, that must be true." She laughed and said that sounded right. And off she went.

Several weeks later when I saw her again, she had a big smile on her face. "Pastor Ray, you won't believe what happened. I was talking with a friend about things, and my friend asked me if I had ever considered going to the mission field. I said no, and she said I should think about it. But I'm a music librarian. What would I do on the mission field? Still, a few days later I happened to pass by a missions display and saw a representative sitting there. Normally I would just walk right by, but this time I stopped to talk. When I asked if they ever needed librarians on the mission field, the man said, 'Absolutely! We could use some librarians right now.' So I started doing some research, and on a Web site I discovered a Christian school in Kenya that needed a librarian starting exactly when I finish my job at Moody. I E-mailed them; they E-mailed back; and they checked my references. And guess what, Pastor Ray? I got the job! I'm moving to Nairobi, Kenya, in late July to get started as the librarian for a Christian school." (As I write these words, she is beginning her third year there and is extremely happy in her work.)

Not long after that, the young couple came back to see me with similar good news. "We're going to Russia." "No kidding. Russia, that's great. Did you know about this when you came to see me?" "No, we had no idea." "So where in Russia are you going?" "We're going to the Black Sea." "That's fantastic. What are you going to do there?" "We're going to teach in a school and help with church planting." When I asked them how they ended up going to the Black Sea to teach and do church planting, they told me a story that was so detailed that it was positively Byzantine in its complexity. They met someone who knew someone who "happened" to know a woman whom they met almost by chance. She came over to talk to them, and one thing led to another, and now there were going to Russia. I couldn't draw it on a chart if I tried, but they were so happy about it and I was happy for them. (As I write these words, they are in language school and soon will be starting their ministry near the Black Sea, teaching and helping plant churches.)

I am amazed as I think about how God led that young woman and that young couple to Kenya and Russia, respectively. But on second thought, why be amazed? That's how God works, isn't it? When you need to know, you'll know. Not one day sooner, not one day later. And if today you don't know what to do next, it's because you truly don't need to know. Because if you needed to know, you would know. If God is God, that must be true.

Psalm 119:105 declares that God's Word is a lamp to our feet and a light to our path. Imagine a man making his way on a dark night through a dangerous forest. There are robbers in the area and wild animals prowling in the darkness. The only light he has comes from the light of the lantern in his hand. With that light he can see just enough to take the next step. As he steps into the light that he has, the light moves forward, and he can see the next step in front of him. He can't see two steps or three or four or five. Only the next step is illuminated. And as he walks into the light, it moves forward, showing him the safe path through the darkness. This is how God leads his children. Always one step at a time. As we walk into the light we have, the light moves forward, and we can see the next step to take.

Are you ready to follow God and to take the next step no matter where it may lead you?
Check your response.
_____ I'm not sure.
_____ No, I need to know everything in advance.
_____ Yes, I'm willing to take that step in faith and leave the results in God's hands.

Living by Faith in Christ

Following Christ can be risky business. You may wonder if everything will work out right if you follow Jesus. It depends on what you think the "right" outcome is.

"Let's Roll"

Millions of people were deeply moved by the story of Todd Beamer, one of the heroes of United Airlines Flight 93 that crashed into the Pennsylvania countryside on September 11, 2001. Speaking to a telephone operator, Todd reported that the plane had been hijacked. Cell phone calls by other passengers brought the news of other hijacked planes crashing into the World Trade Center and the Pentagon. Slowly the frightened passengers pieced it all together. They were never going to get off that plane alive. In a sense, they were already as good as dead. The only question that remained was, Would they fight back? While he was on the phone, Todd asked the operator to recite the Lord's Prayer with him. Then he said, "God help me. Jesus help me." Turning to his fellow passengers, he uttered those now-famous words: "Are you ready? Let's roll." Putting down the phone, he and the other men walked down the aisle toward the cockpit, ready to face their destiny. It was fitting that Todd prayed the Lord's Prayer because it contains the phrase, "Your will be done, on earth as it is in heaven." *Your will be done.* Four simple words, easy to say, but oh so hard to put into practice. Was Todd Beamer in the will of God when he boarded that plane? Yes. Was he in the will of God when he made that phone call? Yes. Was he in the will of God when he and the other passengers walked toward the cockpit, knowing they would soon die? Absolutely. The heroes of Flight 93 died in a fiery crash a few minutes later, but they saved the heart of the nation. Todd Beamer prayed, "Your will be done," and his prayer was answered. Did it work out all right for him? I think from heaven he would answer yes.

"Nothing Bad Happened to Them"

In April 2001, missionaries Jim and Roni Bowers and their children, Corey and Charity, were shot out of the sky by a Peruvian jet that mistook them for drug traffickers. Of all the bullets that were fired that day, a single bullet pierced the fuselage of the missionary airplane, hit Roni in the back and entered the head of seven-month-old Charity, killing them both instantly. Speaking of that terrible moment, Jim Bowers said, "Nothing bad happened to them. They got to heaven quicker than we did." Is that faith or fantasy talking? I submit that those are the words of a man of faith who, out of great personal loss, has "seen him who is invisible," and the sight has transformed his life. Even the worst tragedy doesn't appear that way when viewed from heaven's perspective.

I think we can safely draw three conclusions about those who live by faith:

1. They will see great triumphs and endure great trials.
2. They will be misunderstood by the world.
3. They will be glad they did what they did in the end.

Our call is not to understand but to follow Christ wherever he leads, whatever it costs. And the Word of Christ to all of us is always the same: "Come, follow me" (Matt. 19:21). Try it out. Come to him. Put your life in his hands.

To be a disciple of Christ means to get on the "Jesus road" and follow wherever it takes you. No guarantees, no deals, no special promises. You simply walk that road every day, following in your Master's steps. Don't be afraid to follow Jesus. You'll never regret starting down the "Jesus road." You'll only regret that you waited so long to do it. Are you ready to follow Jesus wherever he leads? That's all he wants. Someone may ask, "What if Jesus asks me to do something I can't do?" He will! He will! He will! If he only asked you to do something you could do, you wouldn't need him. I promise you this: *If you decide to follow Jesus, he will ask you to do the impossible, and then he will help you do it.*

Our part is simply to take the next step. Just take the next step God puts in front of you. You don't have to see the whole plan or even see ten steps down the road. Faith means taking the next step in front of you and leaving the rest in the hands of God.

Faith is the law of the kingdom. And active faith releases God's power. Every blessing of the kingdom is available to those who

put their faith to work, moment by moment, day by day, one little step at a time.

By faith Noah . . .

By faith Abraham . . .

By faith Moses . . .

I wonder if other names could be added to that list. "By faith Elizabeth." "By faith Carlos." "By faith Seth." "By faith Alex." "By faith Karen." "By faith Ray." May God give us steady courage to follow the Lord so that someday our names might be added to the long list of men and women who lived and died by faith.

Active faith releases God's power. This is the Fifth Law of the Spiritual Life.

GOING DEEPER

1. Using Hebrews 11:1 as a starting point, write out your own definition of faith. Ask God to make this definition an ever-increasing reality in your life.

2. Since this chapter argues that "active faith" releases God's power, survey Hebrews 11 to discover how faith moved each person to action. How did God respond in each case to faith in action?

3. What are some ways Christian parents can teach their children to live by faith?

4. In many parts of the world it takes enormous courage for a new believer to be baptized. In what way is baptism an important step in our obedience to Christ? Have you ever been baptized as a believer?

5. According to Romans 10:17, what is the source of our faith? Why is a commitment to the Word of God absolutely essential if you are going to grow in your faith?

6. What is the hardest thing for which you've ever had to trust God? Why was it so difficult? Where is your faith being stretched right now?

CHAPTER 6

The Sixth Law:
There Is No Growth without Struggle

*L*IFE is hard.

Does anyone reading these words have any question about that? I didn't think so. Because we live in a fallen world, nothing works the way it's supposed to. *Sin has stained every part of the physical universe.* And sin has deeply infected the human bloodstream. Things break. Our bodies wear out. We grow old and die. People kill each other. Snipers go on killing sprees. Terrorists blow up buses in the Middle East and fly planes into skyscrapers in America. Marriages break up. Children get hooked on drugs or alcohol or sex—or all three. Babies are born with defects that cannot be corrected. Priests molest children. Pastors commit adultery. Our friends disappoint us. And we disappoint our friends. One day we wake up to find out we're being sued by a former colleague. Or the boss decides that we aren't the right "fit," whatever that means.

Should Christians Suffer?

"Into each life some rain must fall." There is a world of truth in that old adage. No one gets a free ride; no one gets an exemption from pain and sorrow, not even those who commit themselves to walk the Jesus road. *The Sixth Law of the Spiritual Life brings us face-to-face with a reality that some Christians would rather not talk about.* There is abroad in the land today the notion that the Christian life is easy. It isn't. Whoever said that it was? Jesus did say that his yoke is easy and his burden is light, but that was in comparison to the Pharisees, and anyway, an easy yoke is a yoke nonetheless. Jesus also talked about taking up your cross daily, denying yourself, and following him. Nothing easy about that.

The Best Life There Is

Lest I be misunderstood, I hasten to say that *the Christian life is the best life there is because it's the only true life.* To know Christ is to know God, and to know God is to have eternal life. Jesus himself said that anything you give up will be repaid many times over in this life and much more in the life to come (see Mark 10:29–30). The paradox is this: *If you follow Christ, you have to lose your life in order to save it.* You have to go to the cross every day in order to discover the power of the resurrection. You die in order to find abundant life. You reckon yourself dead to sin in order to experience the fullness of life in Christ. None of this is easy to do. If you think it's easy, it's only because you haven't taken the Bible seriously. Romans 7 speaks of a "war" going on in the inner life of the believer, and Romans 8:13 commands us to "put to death" the deeds of the flesh. *Traditionally, Christians have spoken of three great enemies they face: the world, the flesh, and the devil.* The world is "out there" and all around us. The "flesh" is inside and loves to answer the call of the world. And it seems like the devil is everywhere, "like a roaring lion, looking for someone to devour" (1 Pet. 5:8).

No wonder the Bible says that "through many tribulations we must enter the kingdom of God" (Acts 14:22, ESV). And that's why Paul told Timothy to "share in suffering as a good soldier of Christ Jesus" (2 Tim. 2:3, ESV). The hymn "Amazing Grace" contains a verse that teaches this same truth:

Through many dangers, toils and snares,
I have already come.
'Tis grace has brought me safe thus far,
And grace will lead me home.

Truly, there are "many dangers, toils and snares" along the road that leads to heaven. The Sixth Law reminds us that those *difficulties are placed in our path for our spiritual benefit.* This law teaches us that spiritual growth is possible and necessary, but it is not instant or easy. There are no shortcuts on the road to glory. As football coaches love to repeat during those long, hot preseason practices: "No pain, no gain."

Here are four principles that help us think clearly about our trials:

1. Because we live in a fallen world, bad things happen to all of us.

2. We have no control over many things that happen to us or to those around us.

3. We do have complete control over how we respond.

4. Our response to our trials largely determines our spiritual growth—or lack thereof.

If you flip the Sixth Law over, it looks like this: *Struggle in the Christian life is inevitable, lifelong, and ultimately beneficial.* We encounter God's grace through our trials in ways that would not happen if the trials had not come in the first place. It takes a mature Christian to understand this principle, and ironically, it is this principle that makes us mature.

How would your life be changed if you came to regard your struggles as gifts from God meant for your benefit rather than burdens to be carried or punishments to be endured?

_____

_____

_____

_____

"In this you greatly rejoice, though now for a little while you may have had to suffer grief in all kinds of trials. These have come so that your faith—of greater worth than gold, which perishes even though refined by fire—may be proved genuine and may result in praise, glory and honor when Jesus Christ is revealed."
(1 Peter 1:6–7)

Be a Student, Not a Victim

Years ago, my friend Jim Warren (longtime host of *Primetime America* on the Moody Broadcasting Network) passed along this bit of advice: "Ray, when hard times come, be a student, not a victim." The more I have pondered those simple words, the more profound they seem to me. Many people are professional victims, always talking about how unfair life is. A victim says, "Why did this happen to me?" A student says, "I don't care why it happened. I want to learn what God is trying to teach me." A victim looks at everyone else and cries out, "Life isn't fair!" A student looks at life and says, "What happened to me could have happened to anybody." A victim feels so sorry for himself that he has no time for others. A student focuses on helping others so that he has no time to feel sorry for himself. A victim begs God to remove the problems of life so that he might be happy. A student has learned through the problems of life that God alone is the source of all true happiness.

This principle helps answer a question all of us have asked at one time or another: Why is it taking me so long to get better? We've all wondered about that, haven't we?

- "I thought by now I wouldn't struggle so much with anger. Why is it taking me so long to get better?"
- "I still get tempted by pornography. Why is it taking me so long to get better?"
- "I go to church every Sunday, but I still have so many doubts. Why is it taking me so long to get better?"
- "I thought I'd be a better person by now, but I've got so many bad habits. Why is it taking me so long to get better?"
- "I'm a bitter person even though I cover it up most of the time. Why is it taking me so long to get better?"

Many of us wish we had an answer to that question. We might have assumed that upon conversion, we would rapidly sprout wings and fly to heaven. But it doesn't happen that way. *God has ordained that even though we are being made like Jesus, it only happens a little bit at a time.* And sometimes that "little bit" seems very little indeed. When the children of Israel entered the Promised Land, God did not allow them to conquer it all at once. Because there were many entrenched enemies in the hills of Canaan, the Jews had to fight for every inch of it. Then they had to fight to keep what they conquered. It took them many years to possess the entire land. I believe this is a picture of the Christian life. *There is victory to be had, but it will not come easily or quickly.* We are in a warfare with spiritual foes who will not easily yield their ground. Whether we wish to admit it or not, we will struggle with sin and temptation as long as we live. There is no reprieve from this struggle. And that's one major reason why it takes so long for any of us to get better.

Struggle Is Normal

Consider the words of Galatians 5:17: "For the flesh sets its desire against the Spirit, and the Spirit against the flesh; for these are in opposition to one another, so that you may not do the things that you please" (NASB). There is a sense in which struggle is a normal part of the Christian life. Many Christians prefer not to hear this truth because they want a Christianity that proclaims "all victory all the time." They want a guarantee that all their problems will be solved if they will follow the right formula. But that is not realistic, nor is it biblical. We are to fight the good fight of faith, putting on the whole armor of God, standing in the evil day, and enduring hardship as good soldiers of Jesus Christ. Verse 17 is abundantly clear in this regard. Two principles are at war within us. One is called "flesh." The other is called "the Spirit." These two principles are in constant, unrelenting, unremitting antagonism to each other. They are constantly at war with each other. *The flesh* is Paul's term for the depraved nature inside all of us by virtue of our physical descent from Adam. That depraved nature is hostile to God, selfish, and utterly evil. When we come to Christ, we become new creations by virtue of the Holy Spirit who comes to live within us. Even though the dominating power of the flesh has been broken, the pull of evil remains with us. As one writer put it, evil desires arise from the flesh like smoke from a chimney. To say it another way, flesh is what we are by natural birth; the Spirit comes to us by our spiritual birth.

I draw several conclusions from this:

1.   Flesh and the Spirit are fundamentally opposite. They do not and cannot cooperate.

2.   The conflict between our flesh and the Spirit is continual and inevitable.

3.   That conflict produces conflicting desires in the believer.

Thus, with the same mouth we curse and we bless. We love and we hate. We serve, and then we steal. We proclaim Christ, and then we lie to our friends. We read the Bible, and then we watch dirty movies. We sing in the choir, and then we have an affair. And so it goes. The manifestations differ, but all of us feel the struggle in one way or the other.

Some people think, "If I come to Christ, all my problems will be solved. I'll never struggle again." Think again! *If you come to Christ, your problems are just starting.* As a lost person, you sin because that's your nature. As a Christian, you have a new nature that pulls you toward God while the flesh remains with you until you die. In one sense, Christians have conflicts the unsaved never know about. Our rewards are great, but so are our struggles.

We ought to praise God for the war within. *The deadly feud between flesh and Spirit is one sign that we are the children of God.* Do you desire to be holy? Do you want to please the Lord? Is there a hunger in your heart to know Jesus and to love him? Do you desire to live a higher and better life even though you cannot seem to attain it? If you answer yes, that is strong evidence you are born again. Despite your personal failings, do you truly want to do what God wants you to do? Then you may rest in the knowledge that you are a child of God. *Your struggle with sin is proof of your divine heritage.* If sin is a burden, at least it is a burden and not a joy. If you can swear and hate and steal and mock and lust and think all sorts of foul thoughts and speak harsh words, if you can do that and feel nothing, then you are truly without hope in the world.

A Letter from a Young Man

I was given a copy of a letter by a young man I do not know and have never met. Several years ago he graduated from a Christian college. During his days on that campus, he was known and respected as a godly man. I personally know someone whose life was positively impacted by his example. The letter I was given was an open letter he wrote to his friends in which he declared that he had lost his faith and was writing to announce that he was coming "out of the closet" as an active homosexual.

As I read his letter, I was struck by one word that appeared six times in various forms in his letter. The word is *struggle*. The young man spoke of his "struggle" with sexual temptation, his "struggles" with his feelings, his "struggles" to live the Christian life, and in the end, his "struggle" with life itself. Finally he decided that the struggle was not worth the effort, so he decided to stop struggling and to give in. So now he is "in the lifestyle," with all that that phrase implies. As he came to the end of his letter, he asked his friends to accept his decision and not to quote Bible verses or try to "convert" him. He wants to keep his friendships as long as his friends will accept him as a homosexual. He closed his letter with this sentence: "I am finally being true to myself, and I have never been more at peace."

A few comments are in order:

First, he is wrong on both points. By turning to homosexuality, he is only deceiving himself. And any "peace" he now feels is merely the calm before the storm. The Bible says that "the way of transgressors is hard" (Prov. 13:15, KJV). "There is a way that seems right to a man, but its end is the way of death" (Prov. 14:12, NKJV). "Be sure your sin will find you out" (Num. 32:23, NASB). No one gets away with sin forever. At best it offers a temporary respite from the inner turmoil, but it is a false peace that leads to something much worse.

Second, this young man has fallen victim to some very bad theology. Somewhere along the way, he picked up the idea that struggle is bad and that the way to deal with feelings of sexual temptation is to end the struggle by giving in to the temptation. In some ways this is the inevitable result of faulty teaching about the "victorious Christian life." Too much contemporary teaching on this topic seems to imply (if not to state directly) that a Christian may reach a place or a state where the struggles of life disappear altogether. *Such teaching is both false and unbiblical.* It is also dangerous because by promising what it can never deliver, it sets Christians up for failure and immense discouragement when they cannot achieve the promised "victory" over sin. It is only a short jump from this wrong teaching to the conclusion that Christianity itself must be false since the struggles of life continue. Certainly this young man expected some sort of deliverance from his feelings and temptations, which never came. His solution, while radical, exposes the weakness of a theology that seems to promise a "victory" that somehow rarely happens.

Third, the deeper issue is that this young man is using his struggles as an excuse to indulge his fleshly desires. We wouldn't accept his excuse in any other area of life. Suppose a man said, "I have a terrible problem with cursing and bad language. I love to use dirty words and to utter blasphemies. For years I've struggled to control my tongue, but I have often lost the battle. I'm tired of struggling, so I've decided to stop struggling and start cursing all the time. If you want to remain my friend, you'll have to accept my foul mouth and my blasphemies. That's just the way I am. And I feel at peace about my decision." We wouldn't accept an argument like that.

Or suppose a man said, "I love to rob banks. For years I've dreamed about being like Bonnie and Clyde or Butch Cassidy and the Sundance Kid. It seems like a lot of fun. I love the challenge of breaking into a bank and walking out with a lot of money. I've fought the urge to rob banks, but I'm tired of fighting it. I want my friends to know that I'm a bank robber, and I have peace about it." We wouldn't buy that for a second. The point is, we wouldn't accept this sort of sentimental nonsense in any other area, but when someone says, "I'm a homosexual," we're supposed to say, "That's OK." But it's not OK. God has already spoken, and he has not stuttered. Those who ignore his Word do so at their own peril.

Struggling vs. Sinning

Our ongoing struggles and temptations are not in themselves sinful. We are not condemned because we struggle. *It's not the struggle that matters; it's how we respond.* The sin is in giving in, not in the fight itself.

No one escapes the conflict.

No one can avoid the struggle between the flesh and the Spirit.

No one gets a Christian life free from outward pressure and inward turmoil.

There is no second blessing or spiritual experience that can magically propel us to a state where we no longer struggle with sin. That won't happen until we finally get to heaven. Between now and then, we walk the hard road to glory, fighting every day to stay on the right path.

In the end it is impossible to remain neutral. *The Holy Spirit can only help us when we depend on him.* We still have a choice to make: Flesh or Spirit! Right or wrong! Good or evil! My way or God's way!

Why the Struggle Is Good for Us

It's crucial to remember that God allows the struggle as part of our ongoing spiritual growth. *Strange as it may seem, we need to struggle because that's the only way we can grow in grace.* We benefit because struggles:

- reveal to us our inherent weakness.
- kill our pride and arrogance.
- humble us again and again.
- force us to cry out to God for help.
- reveal the uselessness of human effort apart from God's strength.
- teach us to rely on the Lord alone.
- cause us to love the Savior who delivers us from sin.
- lead us to a life of continual repentance.
- make us more watchful against the encroachment of sin.
- make us long for the rest of heaven.
- prod us to use all the means of divine grace.
- encourage us to develop habits of holiness.
- force us to lean on our brothers and sisters to help us out.
- lead us to look for daily solutions instead of instant miracles.

What other benefits of struggle would you add to the above list?

_____

_____

_____

_____

"Finally, be strong in the Lord and in his mighty power. Put on the full armor of God so that you can take your stand against the devil's schemes." (Ephesians 6:10–11)

As we think about the challenge of using our struggles as an avenue for spiritual growth, we can find a great deal of help from James 1:2–4. Here is truth that will help us be students and not victims when hard times come our way.

The Command

"Consider it pure joy, my brothers, whenever you face trials of many kinds" (James 1:2). James begins by reminding us that sooner or later (probably sooner) we will all face trials of various sorts. The word *face* conveys the idea of falling or stumbling over a problem.[1] Picture someone driving down the highway in a convertible. The top is down, the music is blaring, and the driver is having a blast. Not a problem in the world, not a care or a concern. Suddenly there is a bump, a jolt, and the car comes to a sudden halt. What happened? The car hit a massive pothole and suddenly the happy journey is over. *Life is like that for all of us.* No matter who we are or where we live, trouble is just a phone call away. A doctor may say, "I'm sorry. You've got cancer." Or the voice may inform you that your daughter has just been arrested. Or you may be fired without warning. Or someone you trusted may start spreading lies about you. Or your husband may decide he doesn't want to be married anymore. The list is endless because our trials are "multicolored" or "variegated" (the Greek word used for trials has this idea behind it). Unlike the famous ice cream store, our trials come in more than thirty-two varieties.

How, then, should we respond to the hard times that suddenly come to us? James offers what appears to be a strange piece of advice: "Consider it pure joy" or "Count it all joy" (KJV). *That sounds so odd that one wonders if James is serious.* "Count it all joy? Are you nuts? Do you have any idea what I've just been through?" It does sound rather idealistic, if not downright impossible. I confess to being bothered by this, so I decided to check it out in the Greek. No help there. The word *joy* means . . . joy. Pretty simple. So I decided to check out some other translations. One version says, "Be very glad" and another says, "Consider yourselves fortunate" (TEV). That didn't help at all, so I turned to the translation of J. B. Phillips, hoping for some light (if not a way of escape). This is how he handles verse 2: "When all kinds of trials and temptations crowd into your lives, my brothers, don't resent them as intruders, but welcome them as friends!" Even as I type these words, there is a rueful smile on my face. I think it's the exclamation point at the end that does it for me. It's not just "welcome them as friends," which would be hard enough, but "welcome them as friends!" which to me sounds positively giddy, like I'm welcoming long-lost friends to my home.

A "Supernatural" Response

As I have pondered the matter and considered my own difficulties with this concept, the thought occurs that "counting it all joy" when troubles come is not a natural response. If we want a natural response, we can talk about anger or despair or complaining or getting even or running away. It isn't "natural" to find joy in hardship. But that's the whole point. James isn't talking about a "natural" reaction. He's talking about a "supernatural" reaction made possible by the Holy Spirit who enables us to see and to respond from God's point of view. I conclude, then, that *counting it all joy is a conscious choice we make when hard times come.* Truthfully, it's probably a choice we'll have to make again and again and again. And to do it we'll have to take the long view of life, to understand that what we see is not the final chapter of the story. If we can make the choice to view life that way, then we can make the following statements about our struggles and our trials:

1. This is sent from the Lord.
2. This is necessary for my spiritual growth.

The first statement reflects a high view of God's sovereignty. Everything that happens to us is either caused by God or sent by God. If I truly believe that, then I can move to the second statement and begin to look for ways to grow spiritually.

Here's a practical hint. *Don't trust your feelings!* When those you love are in great pain or when you face senseless tragedy or when friends turn against you or when life tumbles in around you, your feelings won't be an accurate guide. You won't "feel" joyful or grateful or full of trust normally. You are quite likely to be filled with a whole bag of negative emotions. So don't judge your circumstances by your feelings. *Judge your circumstances by the Holy Spirit and by the Word of God.* When you do, a powerful conclusion emerges: "These great trials give me great hope that God means a great benefit to me." Seeing things God's way doesn't cancel your trials and it doesn't turn them into nontrials, but it does transform your evaluation of those trials. You will view them differently because you believe that God intends through them to give you a great benefit that could not come any other way.

I read about a pastor in Florida who occasionally throws "count it all joy" parties. He prepares a nice invitation, sends it out to lots of people, and then waits for the response. "Why are you having this party? Is it your birthday? Your anniversary? Did you get a raise?" they ask him. "No, I'm having this party because I'm going through a hard time right now and I want to celebrate because I know God has something good planned for me in the end." The thought occurred to me that this is a far better idea than the "pity parties" many of us like to throw. Perhaps a group of people going through hard times should come together to throw a "count it all joy" party so they can commiserate and celebrate together. That's at least approaching the spirit of our text.[2]

Joy Because God Is in Control

No doubt our main problem comes because we misunderstand the word *joy*. In contemporary parlance, the word is virtually a synonym for happiness. Joy to many people speaks of a pep rally or a champagne party or a New Year's Eve bash. To us, joy means the absence of all pain. But that's not at all what the Bible means. Here's a working definition: *Joy is deep satisfaction that comes from knowing that God is in control even when my circumstances seem to be out of control.* The key to joy is knowing that God is in control. If you know that, you can be satisfied at a very deep level even while you weep over what is happening around you and to you.

During a Bible study on this topic, a friend pointed me to the story of the death of David's son in 2 Samuel 12. You probably remember the details. David seduced Bathsheba, committed adultery with her, and had her husband, Uriah the Hittite, murdered. Then he married her, and all seemed to be well. But the

Lord was displeased with David's sin, so he sent Nathan the prophet to tell David that the child conceived through their adultry would die. When the child was born, the Lord struck him with a serious illness (see v. 15). In response, David fasted and prayed and cried out to God to spare the baby. David lay on the ground weeping for seven days. His servants begged him to eat, but he refused. When the child died on the seventh day, the servants were afraid to tell David because they feared that he might harm himself, so great was his anguish. But David overheard their whispers and asked, "Is the child dead?" When they replied that he was dead, David rose, washed and anointed himself, put on fresh clothes, and went to the temple to worship. Later he returned to his house and began to eat a meal. His puzzled servants couldn't figure out why he fasted and wept when the child was alive, but when he died, he got up, went to the temple, and ate a meal. David's response is classic. He told them that he had fasted and prayed while the child was alive, thinking that God might yet spare him. But once the child died, fasting would make no difference. "Can I bring him back again? I shall go to him, but he shall not return to me" (v. 23, NKJV). The last phrase, by the way, gives us an early glimmer in the Old Testament of the hope of being reunited with our loved ones after death.

You can search through 2 Samuel 12 and you won't find the word *joy* anywhere. *Yet I believe this passage offers us a sad and true-to-life example of what it means to "count it all joy" even in the midst of a terrible personal loss.* There is no laughter here, only pain and sorrow and weeping over one man's foolish choices that led to the death of a son. But David's response teaches us that down deep, far deeper than his sin, he understood God. He wept and prayed and fasted while that was appropriate. When the time had passed, he rose, washed, worshiped, and ate a meal. *He understood that even through his tears, life must go on.* He could not and should not fast and pray and weep forever. There is a time to weep and there is a time to refrain from weeping (see Eccles. 3:1–8).

Sorrow Can Be Selfish

The great nineteenth-century preacher Alexander MacLaren points out that excessive grief can be selfish:

There are many of us who make some disappointment, some loss, some grief, the excuse for shirking plain duty. There is nothing more selfish than sorrow, and there is nothing more absorbing unless we guard against its tendency to monopolize. Work! Work for others, work for God is our best comforter next to the promise of God's Holy Spirit. There is nothing that so lightens the weight of a lifelong sorrow as to make it the stimulus to a lifelong devotion; and if our patience has its perfect work, it will not make us sit with folded hands, weeping for the days that are no more, but it will drive us into heroic and energetic service, in the midst of which there will come some shadow of consolation or, at least, some blessed oblivion of sorrow.[3]

How to Respond Properly to Struggles

And so I ask this practical question: How can we go on when sorrow has paid us a visit? What shall we do when tragedy strikes and we feel like giving up? Here are five suggestions.

A. *Remind Yourself of the Promises of God*

That simply means, dwell much in the Word of God. Talk to yourself and forcibly call to mind the promises of God's presence, his comfort, his divine care, and his unerring purpose to mold you into the likeness of his Son. In the darkest hours, the promises will not come easily. You must do whatever it takes to feed your own soul with the Bread of Life.

B. *Search for Opportunities to Give Thanks to God*

There are times when thanksgiving seems almost impossible and sometimes even impious. Sin, in all its ugliness, sometimes comes as an unwanted guest. Should we give thanks for sin? No, never. But even if you cannot give thanks for 99 percent of what is happening, focus on the 1 percent you clearly see, and give thanks to God for that.

C. *Refuse to Give In to Bitterness and Despair*

I am speaking here of the conscious choices of the heart. Too many times we speak as if we were involuntarily overwhelmed and had no choice but to be bitter, angry, and hostile. Or we had no choice but to give up our faith in God. Better we should say, "I could give in to anger, but by God's grace I will choose a higher road. I could turn away from my Lord, but I will not do it."

D. *Choose to Believe in God*

That means exactly what it says. Believe in God! Believe in his goodness. Believe in his love. Believe in his kindness. Faith is a choice made by the heart. If you want to believe, you will believe, and the angels of heaven will come to your aid.

E. Make Up Your Mind to Go On with life

This is what David did. This is what we must do. Grief is good and proper and is healing and even ennobling, but after grief has done its work of healing and helping, then we must move on. *The past is gone, and we can't go back.* Don't try. You can't live in yesterday. And you can't even live in today. The voice of God calls us onward toward tomorrow. Several years ago I formulated a principle I call the First Law of Spiritual Progress. It goes like this:

I can't go back.

I can't stay here.

I must go forward.

Even if we want to go back, we can't. And we can't stay where we are. God's call is always onward, forward, moving out by faith into the unknown future. This is not easy, but it must be done. When we do it, we will discover a well of joy springing up to refresh our souls as we march onward with the Lord.

Is God calling you to "go forward" in some area of your life?
 · Thank God for his call on your life.
 · Affirm your confidence that God knows what is best for you.
 · Tell the Lord that you intend to go forward as he leads you step by step.

"For this God is our God for ever and ever; he will be our guide even to the end." (Psalm 48:14)

The Reason for Struggles in the Christian Life

"Because you know that the testing of your faith develops perseverance" (James 1:3). The phrase *you know* in this verse refers not to head knowledge (what we sometimes call "book learning") but to heart knowledge, the kind gained from years of experience. Some things we learn from books; others we learn from daily life in the "school of hard knocks." God puts our faith to the test. The word *testing* refers to the process by which gold ore was purified. In order to separate the gold from the dross, the ore was placed in a furnace and heated until it melted. The dross rose to the surface and was skimmed off, leaving only pure gold. That's a picture of what God is doing in our "fiery trials." We all have to undergo some "furnace time" sooner or later. Some of us will spend an extended time in the furnace of affliction. But the result is the pure gold of Christlike character. Job spoke of this experience when he declared of the Lord: "He knows the way that I take; when he has tested me, I will come forth as gold" (Job 23:10).

What specifically is God trying to do when he allows his children to go through hard trials and deep suffering? There are several answers to that question. *First,* God wants to purge us of sin and to purify us of iniquity. *Second,* God uses suffering to test our faith. Will we still obey God in the darkness? Will we serve God when things aren't going our way? Will we hold on to the truth when we feel like giving up? *Third,* God uses times of difficulty to humble us. When things are going well, we tend to get puffed up about our accomplishments; but let the darkness fall and we are on our knees crying out to God. *Fourth,* God definitely uses hard times to prepare us to minister to others. He comforts us so that we may comfort others. I know many Christians whose greatest ministry has come from sharing with others how God helped them through a time of crisis. *Fifth,* I believe God uses hard times to prepare us for a new understanding of his character. In the furnace we discover God's goodness in a way we never experienced it before.

Until your faith is put to the test, it remains theoretical. *You never know what you believe until hard times come.* Then you find out, for better or for worse. When the phone rings with bad news, when your son winds up in prison, when your best friend betrays you, when you lose your job, when your parents suddenly die, when life comes apart at the seams—then you discover what you truly and actually believe in the depth of your soul. Until then, your faith is speculative because it is untested. You can talk about heaven all you want, but you'll discover whether or not you believe in it when you stand by the casket of someone you love.

God's great design is to produce "perseverance." The Greek word is *hupomone,* sometimes translated as "endurance" or "steadfastness" or "patience." In the Book of Revelation, this word describes the faith of those brave saints who would not take the "mark of the beast" (see Rev. 13:18). *Thus it describes a certain kind of "battle-tested" faith that stands up under withering fire from the enemy and does not cut and run.* Theologian and author William Barclay notes that in the early church the martyrs gained the respect of unbelievers because in the moment of death, they had this quality. To the very end, they died with their faith intact. Of them it was said, "They died singing."[4]

God's Promise

"Perseverance must finish its work so that you may be mature and complete, not lacking anything" (James 1:4). There is a process involved in our trials that leads to a product. *Perseverance requires work and faith and hope and dogged determination to hold on to our faith even when the world seems to be disintegrating around us.* Perseverance says, "I will not give up no matter what happens or how bad life may be. I will hold on because I promised and because I believe the Lord has something in store for me." The reward of such gritty stubbornness is genuine spiritual maturity. When trials have finished their work in us, we will not lack anything the Lord wants us to have. If we need faith, we will have it. If we need hope, we will have it. If we need love, we will have it. If we need any of the ninefold fruit of the Spirit (see Gal. 5:22–23), it will be produced in us. Nothing will be left out; nothing will be left behind.

During my college years I worked briefly at a carpet mill in Chattanooga, Tennessee. My job was fairly low-tech—mostly pushing a broom and keeping the walkways clean. In my spare moments I loved to watch the huge carpet machines at work. As I stood in the back I could see huge spools of yarn—dozens of them, of every conceivable color—spinning rapidly as the yarn went into the machine. From the backside everything seemed to be a meaningless jumble of colors and noise. Nothing made any sense. There didn't seem to be the slightest pattern at work—just a mass of colored threads making their way at high speed into the mechanical weaver. When I walked to the front of the machine, however, an entirely different sight greeted me. There I could see carpet slowly emerging—row by row, all the colors perfectly in place, arranged in order as if by magic. But it wasn't magic at all. Someone had programmed the machine to take that tangle of threads and turn it into a pattern of exquisite beauty.

In this life we stand as if we were at the back of the machine looking at the multicolored threads of circumstance. Some are the dark colors of sadness and confusion; others, the bright tones of happiness and success. On this side there seems to be no pattern—only colors and noise. Now and again God gives us a peek at the finished product, and we are aware that something beautiful is being produced in us by the Master Designer. *But in this life we never see the big picture.* That will all change when we finally get to heaven. Then we will see that everything that happened to us had a purpose—even those things that seemed to bring us nothing but pain and heartache. These dark tones that seem so pointless will in that day be a vital part of a pattern so beautiful that if we were to see it now, it would take our breath away. Let us therefore be patient and let the Master Designer complete his work in us. When we cannot see the big picture, we can still trust that our heavenly Father knows exactly what he is doing. And *while we wait, let us take every open door the Lord gives us to share Christ with those around us.* As we seek first the kingdom of God, we will discover that through the good times and the bad, in days of pleasure and days of pain, through our laughter and through our tears, God is at work in us.

The great danger is that we will try to short-circuit the process by running away from our problems. Eugene Peterson (*The Message*) translates part of James 1:4 this way: "Don't try to get out of anything prematurely." That's good advice, though it's not always easy to follow. We can see the full flowering of this passage in the lives of older saints of God. As I thought about this truth, I recalled Mabel Scheck, who died after a long battle with cancer. Mabel was in her 80s and had been a member of Calvary

Memorial Church for almost sixty years. She and her husband joined our congregation near the end of World War II. He died many years ago, and by the time I met Mabel, she was in her mid-70s. Over the years we became close friends. Mabel was full of vinegar and spice and pep, and she was always ready with a quip or a comment. Almost every Sunday I would tease her, and she would tease me right back. About ten years ago she developed cancer. The doctors did all they could but finally could do no more. She surprised them all by surviving three or four bouts with cancer. I used to kid her that she was living on "bonus time" from the Lord. When the cancer came back for the last time, she was truly ready to go to heaven. No fear, no doubts, and no regrets. Shortly before she died, my wife, Marlene, and I went to visit her. By this time Mabel could barely breathe, and her words were hard to understand. Yet her faith was undiminished. Cancer could take her earthly life, but it could not destroy her walk with God. As she labored to get her breath, in a very faint voice she greeted us and said how glad she was that we had come to see her. She wanted to talk about things at the church and to hear the latest news. "I'm ready to go whenever the Lord wants to take me home," she said. Then she added, "The Lord has been so good to me." A few days later I spoke at her funeral service.

When I think of Mabel Scheck at the end of her life, two words come to mind: *Pure Gold.* Through long years of difficulty, God had fashioned truly Christlike character in her. She was mature and complete; nothing was lacking. I think that's what James means when he says in 1:3, "You know." We know these things are true because we have learned them by experience and because we have seen them come true in the lives of others.

Things Known and Unknown

Let me wrap up this chapter with a few concluding words. When trials come (and they will come to all of us eventually), there is something we can't know and something we can know.

We can't always know *why things happen the way they do.*

No matter how hard we try to figure things out, there will always be many mysteries in life. *The greater the tragedy, the greater will be the mystery.* God does not explain himself to us. As we go through life, we can look back and see many blanks that we wish God would fill in for us. Most of the time we will carry those unfilled blanks with us all the way to heaven.

When hard times come, we can know *that God is at work in our trials for our benefit and for his glory.*

To say that is to say nothing more than the words of Romans 8:28: "And we know that in all things God works for the good of those who love him." For the children of God, "all things" do indeed work together for good. Sometimes we will see it; often we will simply have to take it by faith. But it is true whether we believe it or not. And so we are left with the simple words of the Sixth Law of the Spiritual Life: *There is no growth without struggle.* As long as we live in a fallen world, we cannot fight against this law and win. Your arms are too short to box with God.

Be of Good Cheer!

When Charles Simeon finished his exposition of James 1:2–4, he addressed himself to two groups of people. *First, there are the timid, those who fear the trials of life.* Our message is: Be of good cheer. Fear not. Nothing can touch you that does not first pass through the hands of your heavenly Father. Though the arrow be shot by the evil one, it cannot touch you unless God wills it so. And your Father who loves you will never give you more than you can bear. Though you may feel that you are far past the limit, you aren't. God measures his trials along with his blessings. If he afflicts you, it is not to destroy you but to develop in you the gold of Christlike character.

Second, there are those who are suffering right now. Should we pity those who are passing through the fires of difficulty at this very moment? No! *We should rather congratulate them that God has counted them worthy of such great trials.* Nothing is wasted—not pain, tears, confusion or even doubts. All of it is grist for the mill of God's loving purpose. "Behind a frowning providence, he hides a smiling face." Receive with joy what God has given you, and bless his name.[5]

Two Simple Words

In order to make all we have talked about as simple as possible, I'd like to boil everything down to just two words. When hard times come, when trials fall upon us (or we seem to fall upon them), when the slings and arrows of outrageous fortune knock us to the ground, what should we do? Remember these two words:

Pray and *Stay.*

As you read this, stop right now and say these two words out loud: *Pray* and *Stay.* Now write them down on a piece of paper in big letters: *PRAY* and *STAY.*

Don't run. Don't hide. Don't shake your fist at God. Don't start arguing with the Almighty. Don't waste time trying to make excuses or empty promises. And don't try to bargain your way out of trouble. It doesn't work, and you don't have anything to bargain with anyway.

Pray and stay. Pray and stay. Pray and stay.

Pray: Seek God's face. Spend time with the Lord. Listen for his voice. Ask God, "What are you trying to teach me? Speak, Lord, and I will listen to your voice."

Stay: Wait. Be patient. Don't rush God. (You can't rush him anyway!) Refuse to run away. Affirm by faith that God is at work even though he seems invisible and your life seems chaotic.

Don't do anything foolish or hasty. While I was having lunch with an old friend recently, he reminded me that years ago he came to talk to me because his marriage was falling apart. In fact, he had made up his mind that he was going to divorce his wife because the situation seemed hopeless. During our discussion, I had asked him one question: "Is there any decision you *need* to make today?" His answer was no. So I told him not to do anything until he had to. Soon after that there was a breakthrough in their situation that led to a turnaround that transformed his wife, himself, and their marriage. My advice to him then applies to us all. If you are tempted to take a quick and easy road out of your troubles, stop a moment and think about it. Do you have to do anything today? Then don't. Give God time to work. There will be time to "do something" later if you have to.

The Choice Is Ours

A TRUTH TO REMEMBER: Strange as it may seem, we need to struggle because that's the only way we can grow in grace.

❧

The Christian way is not an easy way, and any representations to the contrary are false. There is an abundant life to be had, and there is spiritual victory, and there is joy in the Lord and the filling of the Spirit, but those things don't come in spite of our trials. Most often they come through and with and alongside our trials. In various ways we will all struggle every day as we make our earthly pilgrimage. In a fallen world, there can be no other way. For the most part, we can't choose our trials, nor can we avoid most of them. But we can choose how we respond. That part is up to us. We can respond with

joy or bitterness.

forgiveness or anger.

trust or unbelief.

faith or fear.

love or hatred.

kindness or malice.

temperance or self-indulgence.

gentleness or stubbornness.

mercy or revenge.

peace or worry.

hope or despair.

Our perspective makes all the difference. God does not intend to destroy us by the trials he allows to come our way. Those things that seem so painful now will one day be clearly seen as benefits to our spiritual growth. They are not meant to defeat us but to be the means to a greater spiritual victory. Therefore, we should not complain when hard times come. We should rejoice. *And we will rejoice if we believe what God has said.* Every hard trial is another step on the stairway that leads from earth to heaven. While we journey forward, the truth remains: There is no growth without struggle. This is the Sixth Law of the Spiritual Life.

GOING DEEPER

1. Why is it hard for most of us to "count it all joy" when we face hard times? Why is the truth of God's sovereignty absolutely essential to finding joy in the midst of our trials? How does David's reaction to the death of his son in 2 Samuel 12 illustrate this principle?

2. "Your struggle with sin is proof of your divine heritage." According to 1 John 1:10, what are the two negative results of denying our own sinfulness?

3. Ponder the First Law of Spiritual Progress cited on page 158. In what ways are you tempted to "go back" even though you know you must "go forward" with God?

4. Can you think of others like Mabel Scheck, whose faith seemed to grow stronger in spite of intense personal suffering? What lessons have you learned from their example?

5. "I am finally being true to myself, and I have never been more at peace." How would you respond to the young man who wrote the letter mentioned in "A Letter from a Young Man"?

6. In what area of your life is God calling you to "pray and stay" right now?

CHAPTER 7

The Seventh Law:
What God Starts,
He Finishes

We BEGIN WITH THE WORDS OF DIETRICH BONHOEFFER, the German pastor whose opposition to Adolph Hitler during World War II not only landed him in jail, but brought his death at the hand of the Nazis shortly before the end of the war. Bonhoeffer's best-known writings include *The Cost of Discipleship* and *Life Together.* At one point he pondered what it means to live in wartime while still believing in the promises of God. These are his words: "There remains for us only the very narrow way, often extremely difficult to find, of living every day as though it were our last, and yet living in faith and responsibility as though there were to be a great future."[1] There have been, and will be, moments in history when living each day as if it were our last is literally the only way we can live.

A few months after the terrorist attacks on September 11, 2001, Peggy Noonan wrote a column for the *Wall Street Journal* about the worsening crisis in the Middle East.[2] The article points out that for a long time, most of us have tried not to worry much about the Middle East. We have known that the various parties to the conflict don't like each other, but we have had faith that someone, somewhere, would work out a peace deal to keep the lid on so it wouldn't blow up and start World War III. *Now, in 2003, recent events have destroyed that sort of naïve optimism.* The situation has deteriorated so badly that now no one has the answer. Not even Secretary of State Colin Powell can bring the Palestinians and the Israelis together. In some ways it seems ironic that in a world of such amazing technological advance, we seem utterly unable to bring an end to this ancient hostility.

In her article, Noonan points out that all we can do, all we are really trying to do, is to buy time, to push back the inevitable so that no one detonates a nuclear bomb and wipes out the other side. She further explains that some consider the Middle East to be the vortex of history—where history started and where it will ultimately end. And if God speaks to humanity from the Middle East then his message to us right now is: You are all in a heap of trouble.

Noonan's column ends with a call to prayer. Why pray? Because it's always easier to fight than to pray. Fighting is hard enough, but prayer is much harder because it means giving up the certainty that you have all the answers. When you pray, you are confessing that there is a realm outside this world, and that God—who dwells in eternity—can affect what happens in time. Prayer may be our last, best, and only hope in these troubled times.[3]

Take time now to . . .
  • praise God for his power to deliver us from times of trouble.
  • pray for our national leaders. Ask God to give them the fear of the Lord that leads to wisdom.
  • think of one way you have experienced God's goodness this week. Take a moment to say thank you to the Lord.

"Do not be anxious about anything, but in everything, by prayer and petition, with thanksgiving, present your requests to God."
(Philippians 4:6)

If God Is for Us . . .

We have come to the seventh and final law of the spiritual life. In case you have forgotten them, here are the first six laws:

Law 1: He's God and we're not.

Law 2: God doesn't need us, but we desperately need him.

Law 3: What God demands, he supplies.

Law 4: What you seek, you find.

Law 5: Active faith releases God's power.

Law 6: There is no growth without struggle.

The final law brings us back to God as the source and end of our faith:

Law 7: What God starts, he finishes.

This law gives us hope in hard times and keeps us going when we would rather quit. It's the law that inspired believers to be faithful under persecution and gave Moses the strength to reject the treasures of Egypt in favor of the unseen riches of the invisible God. This law reminds us that *in the end, everything we give up for the Lord will seem like no sacrifice at all.* When life tumbles in around us and others have given up their faith, we can stand firm because we know that what we see is not all there is. The best is yet to come.

As I have pondered this truth, the words of Romans 8:31 have been ringing in my mind: "What, then, shall we say in response to this? If God is for us, who can be against us?" This is the question that the people of the world want answered. Is there a God, and if there is a God, is he for us or against us? When Paul says *if* God is for us, he's not saying maybe he is and maybe he isn't. It can be translated: "Since God is for us" or "Because God is for us." *There is no truth more fundamental in all of God's Word than this truth: God is for us.* God is not against us. God is not neutral toward us. Because of Jesus Christ, once and for all the question is settled. God is for us. *All that God is, all that God has, and all that God does, he does on behalf of his people.* Even those times when God seems to be acting against us, if we could only look behind the veil, we would understand that God is for us.

Name the enemies of the people of God. Can the devil stand against us? No, because he has been defeated. Can the world stand against us? No, because Jesus has overcome the world. Can the flesh destroy us? No, because in Jesus Christ we overcome the pull of the flesh. Therefore, let the people of God be bold. Who dares to stand against us if God be for us?

Three Truths on which You Can Depend

The truth of the Seventh Law depends on several important attributes of God. *First: God is faithful.* That means he does not lie, he does not change in his essential character, and he acts in time and space to ensure that his purposes are carried out. He perseveres until that which he has ordained comes to fruition. There are no gaps and no performance failures with the Lord. He is faithful to himself, to his Word, and to all his creatures. In the end, all things in the universe will be seen to have served God's purposes. No detail will be missing, nothing will be out of place, and there will be no "accidents." Even the tragedies of life will fit into God's eternal plan. The fact that we cannot see how this could be true simply demonstrates the First Law: He's God and we're not. God is faithful whether we see it or not, and he is faithful whether we believe it or not.

Second: God is good. This attribute tells us that God is "for" us and not "against" us. He intends to bless us beyond our expectations, and he desires to even bless those who rebel against him. "You are good, and what you do is good" (Ps. 119:68). Because God is faithful and because he is good, we can be confident that what God starts, he finishes. Sooner or later, his Word will be proved true, his justice will be vindicated, his wisdom will be plainly displayed, and the magnificence of his grace will be placarded from one end of the universe to the other. His Name will be glorified and we will be satisfied.

As we work and wait and hope for that day to come, here are three truths you can depend on.

A. All God's Promises Will Eventually Be Fulfilled

The key word here is *eventually.* While reading through Joshua, I came across some verses that serve as a summary of God's faithfulness to his people. These verses come at the end of the section where the Jews have defeated their enemies and taken possession of the Promised Land. It had been a hard fight, and people died in the process. It took blood, sweat, and tears to conquer the land and drive out the pagan people. But at last the work was done, the tribes had received their allotment, and the nation was ready to settle down and live in peace. Against that background, Joshua offers this assessment: "Thus the LORD gave to Israel all the land that he swore to give to their fathers. And they took possession of it, and they settled there. And the LORD gave them rest on every side just as he had sworn to their fathers. Not one of all their enemies had withstood them, for the LORD had given all their enemies into their hands. Not one word of all the good promises that the LORD had made to the house of Israel had failed; all came to pass" (Josh. 21:43–45, ESV). Note that although the Lord "gave" them the land, they still had to fight for it. Their "rest" came only after long years of warfare. They had to go into battle over and over again, blood had to be shed, and no doubt some soldiers had to die in order for God's promises to come true. It's not as if the Jews "claimed" the promise and simply moved in with no opposition. They had to fight to win what God had promised them.

So it is for you and me. *We must fight the good fight, put on the whole armor of God, and be good soldiers for the Lord.* That means enduring long days and longer nights, facing fears within and foes without, being misunderstood by the world and sometimes by our best friends, living by radically different standards than the people around us, and claiming dual allegiance to two nations—one on earth and the other in heaven. Living for Christ means hard times, bearing the cross, despising the shame, denying ourselves, following him wherever he leads, judging all things by the values of the kingdom, putting others above our own interests, yielding our rights, refusing to give in to anger and rage, forgiving when we'd rather get even, loving our enemies, laying down our lives for others, giving until it hurts and then giving some more, bearing one another's burdens, washing dirty feet, taking on the role of a servant, and sometimes being regarded as fools and scum of the earth. Sometimes we will be opposed, sometimes hated, sometimes mocked, sometimes persecuted, and sometimes the followers of Christ will be put to death. It happens.

The point is, *being a Christian does not exempt you from the problems of life.* Coming to Christ solves some problems and creates others. The problems solved include salvation, eternal life, forgiveness, removal of guilt, provision of a brand-new life, new desires, and new power to serve God. It means a home in heaven and abundant life while you live on earth. So it's not a bad deal. Not at all. The "problems" you gain are rather small in comparison, but they are problems nonetheless. Being a follower of Christ is a wonderful life. It's the best life there is, and it's really the only life there is. Apart from Christ there is no life at all. But it doesn't mean that things will be easy or simple or that life will be a bed of roses. Or maybe it will be a bed of roses, but those roses will have thorns.

The good news is that *God fully intends to keep his promises to you.* What he did for Israel so long ago, he does for his people today. As we trust and obey, as we fight and pray, as we stand up for righteousness and shine light in a darkened world, one by one by one the promises are kept. And in the end (and not until then) we will look back and say, "The Lord did it. Not one of his good promises failed. All came to pass."

B. The Lord Will Complete His Work in Us

Psalm 138:8 says this plainly. "The LORD will fulfill his purpose for me; your steadfast love, O LORD, endures forever" (ESV). The argument here is very simple. Because the Lord's love endures forever, his purposes for us will endure forever. If God's love could somehow fail, then perhaps we could doubt his purposes. But since his love reflects his eternal character, we can be sure that God will do whatever it takes to accomplish whatever he wants to accomplish in us.

C. The Entire Work of Salvation Is Guaranteed by God

Consider Romans 8:29–30. "For those God foreknew he also predestined to be conformed to the likeness of his Son, that he might be the firstborn among many brothers. And those he predestined, he also called; those he called, he also justified; those he justified, he also glorified." Circle or underline the following five words in the above text:

foreknew

predestined

called

justified

glorified

These five words make up the golden chain of your salvation. It is a golden chain of five links. These five words comprehend the entire work of God on your behalf. *No other statement in the Bible so comprehensively contains what God is doing to accomplish your salvation.* He begins in eternity past and finishes in eternity future. To say it another way, your salvation begins in heaven, comes to earth, and ends up in heaven.

Your salvation begins with the first link—foreknowledge. That's the link that starts in heaven. Then we come to predestination. That's the link that brings salvation down to earth. Then we come to calling. That's the link where you are hooked onto the chain. Justification is the link that ensures your righteous standing before the Lord. Glorification is the link that secures your eternal place in heaven. These five things are the five links in the chain of your salvation. *They are true of every believer. They are true only of believers.* If you are a believer, these five links in the chain explain God's plan from eternity past to eternity future to accomplish your salvation.

Notice the tense of the five key words: foreknew, predestined, called, justified, glorified. They are all in the past tense. But how can "glorified" be in the past tense when our glorification is in the future? How can God speak of our future glorification in the past tense if it hasn't even happened yet? The answer is this: *It is so certain that God speaks of it as past tense even though it is still future to us.* In God's mind past, present, and future are all the same. In a sense that we can't fathom, our glorification has already happened. It's so certain that God can speak of it in the past tense.

Let me illustrate: If God foreknew 100 people, then he predestined 100. If God predestined 100, he called 100. If God called 100, he justified 100. If God justified 100, then he glorified 100. It's not as if God starts out with 1,500 people but loses some in the process. It is not as if he foreknows 1,500, then he predestines 1,200, then he calls 800, then he justifies 400, and only has about 60 or 70 left to finally take to heaven. It's not a declining number. The number is exactly the same throughout. *As many as he foreknew in the beginning, exactly that many will he glorify in the end.* So let's suppose the Lord is in heaven counting his sheep: "94 . . . 95 . . . 96 . . . 97 . . . 98 . . . 99 . . . Pritchard, where's Pritchard? I can't find him!" No, it's not like that. Everyone he foreknows, everyone he predestines, everyone he calls, everyone he justifies—all of them eventually will be glorified. No one will be lost in the process.

Youth evangelist Jack Wyrtzen used to say it this way: "I'm as sure of heaven as if I'd already been there ten thousand years." Why? Because it doesn't rest on me. It doesn't rest on you. *It rests on the Word of the eternal God.* If God has said he's going to do it, he will do it. You can book it, you can take it to the bank. What God says he will do, he will do. All of God's sheep will make it. That's good news for all us sheep. Some of God's sheep are sick and weak, some are wayward, and a few are downright rebellious. And some of the sheep have been messing around with the goats too much, and they look more like goats than like sheep. But fear not. The Lord knows his own, he knows how to find his own, and when the time comes, all of God's sheep will make it into the fold. Not one will be lost. Not one.

Seven Ways to Apply the Seventh Law

Let's wrap up this chapter by looking at a few ways we can apply this great truth—that what God starts, he always finishes.

A. We Can Be Certain of Our Salvation

First John 5:12–13 tells us that eternal life is only to be found in Jesus Christ and that those who believe in him may "know" that they have eternal life. *In this world of so much uncertainty, here is something God says you can know.* That's hugely important. Do you want to go to heaven? You can. Do you want to know you're going to heaven? You can. Many people, even many Christians, say, "I hope I'm going to heaven," but that is not the language of the Bible. For those who truly trust Christ, there is a certainty that does not depend on them or their works, but on the promise of God, who cannot lie. Because salvation is God's work, when we trust Christ we can know that we are saved, that our sins are forgiven, that we are right with God, and that should we die tonight, we will go to heaven.

Do you know for certain that if you died tonight, you would go to heaven? Give the basis for your answer in the space below.

_____

_____

_____

_____

"Whoever believes in the Son has eternal life, but whoever rejects the Son will not see life, for God's wrath remains on him." (John 3:36)

B. We Can Be Confident of God's Purposes for Us

This is one of those "long-range" truths that helps us when we are down and discouraged and wonder if we're all that we were truly meant to be. Philippians 1:6 reminds us that "he who began a good work in you will carry it on to completion until the day of Christ Jesus." *This is one of the greatest verses in the entire Bible.* Theologians use it to defend the doctrine of the perseverance of the saints. I don't particularly like that phrase—"the perseverance of the saints"—because it puts the emphasis in the wrong place. I prefer to say that I believe in the *"perseverance* of God" and the *"preservation* of the saints." Philippians 1:6 teaches us that we will be "preserved" to the end because God will always "persevere." What God starts he always finishes.

Note three things from this verse. *First, God takes the initiative in starting his work in you.* He is the one who "begins a good work" in us. Salvation always begins with God. He makes the first move, and if he didn't make the first move, we would make no move at all. Perhaps you've heard of the country preacher who was being examined for his ordination to the ministry. When asked how he had become a Christian, the preacher replied, "I did my part, and God did his." That sounded questionable, so the learned brethren on the council asked the preacher to explain "his part in salvation." "My part was to run from God as fast as I could," the preacher answered. "God's part was to run after me and catch me and bring me into his family." That's a perfectly biblical answer because all of us were born running from God, and unless God took the initiative to find us, we would still be running away from him.

Second, God takes personal responsibility for completing his work in you. I find this a most comforting thought. God has a "good work" that he intends to use in your life and in mine. Nothing will block the accomplishment of that divine purpose. God intends that all his children be conformed to the image of Jesus Christ, and he will not rest until that "good work" is finally finished.

Perhaps you've seen those buttons that read PBPGIFWMY. Those cryptic letters stand for a most important truth: "Please be patient. God isn't finished with me yet." Thank God, it's true. I may not look like much—but God isn't finished with me yet. When you look in the mirror—and even deeper into your own soul—you may not like what you see, but no matter. God isn't finished with you yet. There is good news and bad news in this truth. The good news is that since God isn't finished yet, we have great hope for the future. The bad news is that since God isn't finished yet, he won't let us stay as we are today. He's going to keep chipping away at us until we are conformed to the image of Jesus Christ. Most of us have a long way to go—and some of us have an enormous distance to travel. But it doesn't matter. I'd rather be six inches from hell heading toward heaven than six inches from heaven heading toward hell. Direction makes all the difference.

If you find yourself in the muck and mire of personal defeat as you read these words, be encouraged. Child of God, he's not finished with you yet. Rise and walk, my Christian friend. God is not finished with you yet. If you've been sent to the bench for a personal foul, learn the lesson God has for you and then get back in the game. God's not finished with you yet.

Third, God guarantees the outcome of his work in you. Not only does God start the process and continue the process, he also guarantees its ultimate outcome. He will "carry it on to completion until the day of Christ Jesus." This means that God won't be turned aside by difficulties of any kind. He is so determined to make you like Jesus that even your own backsliding won't ultimately hinder the accomplishment of his purpose. Someday you and I will stand before Jesus Christ as redeemed children of God—holy, blameless, and complete in every way. We're a far sight from that today, but a better day is coming for the people of God. What is incomplete will be made complete. What is unfinished will be finished. What is lacking will be made full. What is partial will be made whole. What is less than enough will be far more than adequate. What is broken will be fixed. What is hurt will be healed. What is weak will be made strong. What is temporary will be made permanent.

God has promised to do it, and he cannot lie. Has God begun a good work in your life? Do you feel incomplete and unfinished? Fear not, child of God. He will complete his work in you.

A young missionary family was forced to leave their home in Zaire because of unrest in the region. Eventually they moved to Nairobi, Kenya. "And what news did we receive upon our arrival? You all know about the deadly bombing at the US embassy here in town. So where are we safer? In God's hands!" Some people might think it reckless to take young children into such a dangerous area of the world, *but Tim and Debra have done it for the sake of the gospel.* Because of their confidence in God, they can go without fear wherever the Lord leads them. Maybe you've seen those T-shirts the kids wear—the ones that say NO FEAR in big letters. If you have confidence in God, you can have NO FEAR as you face whatever comes your way.

C. We Can Have Comfort in the Midst of Confusing Circumstances

Many things in life confuse and perplex us. Things happen, both good and bad, in such seemingly random sequence that

List several areas of your life where you need to say No FEAR right now.

_____

_____

_____

_____

"The LORD is with me; I will not be afraid." (Psalm 118:6)

most of the time we can't begin to understand the big picture. Not long ago the roommate of one of my sons learned that his father had an inoperable brain tumor. It seemed to happen suddenly, without warning and without any apparent reason. The father's last few days were very difficult as the tumor invaded new areas of the brain. A few nights ago the suffering ended, and he went home to be with the Lord. My son wrote an E-mail about how hard it was to see his roommate deal with his father's death. The E-mail ended with these words: "All of this is to an end. . . . It will be good . . . God will be shown through all of this, God is good." There is a profound truth underlying what he wrote. "It will be good." It isn't "good" right now. At least it doesn't seem good or feel good. Any good that is there must be seen and felt and taken by faith. Death is still the last enemy of the people of God. But death isn't the end of the story. *God will be glorified even through things that seem senseless and even evil to us.* We won't always see how this works out in history, but it is true nonetheless. "For we know," Paul says in Romans 8:28. Not "we think" or "we hope" or "we dream," but "we know," as if to state a settled fact, that "all things," not "some things" or "most things" or even "the things that make sense to us" work together for good, to those who love God, who are called according to his purpose. Because God is good, "it will be good," and we will see that goodness somewhere down the road—if not in this life, then in eternity. All will be well, and God will be glorified.

D. We Can Remain Calm When the World Is in Turmoil

I suppose I would not have made this particular application two years ago. But now, after September 11, after anthrax and the threat of bioterrorism, after heightened airport security, after Afghanistan, after the war to liberate Iraq, and in the midst of all the bloodshed in the Middle East, this application seems urgent. Many of the experts believe that further acts of terrorism are not only likely, they are inevitable. Clearly, there are people out there who think nothing of blowing themselves up in the pursuit of their goals. Peace is hard to come by because there is so much hatred and mistrust on every side. We now live in a time of color-coded terror alerts. We must arrive at the airport hours before a flight in order to make it through security.

How will we maintain our sense of balance in a world like this? *Psalm 46 points us back to God—our refuge and strength, a very present help in time of trouble.* The word *help* means that he will be for us whatever we need, whenever we need it. He is the super-natural resource when our strength has come to an end. "Therefore we will not fear, though the earth give way and the mountains fall into the heart of the sea" (v. 2). It is hard to read that verse without remembering the Twin Towers suddenly crumbling to the ground. "Nations are in uproar, kingdom fall" (v. 6). What a fitting description for the current crisis in the Middle East. So, what shall believers do in days of uncertainty? Will we give in to fear and desperation? "Be still, and know that I am God" (v. 10). Be still. Those who know God remain calm even under threat of Armageddon. We know that God is in control. "The LORD Almighty is with us; the God of Jacob is our fortress" (v. 11). As believers, we do not claim any special insight into politics or military matters, and we don't claim to know what will happen in the Middle East. What we do know is this: *Our God is in control.* Therefore we will not fear. We will be still and know that the Lord is God.

E. We Can Trust God with the Details of Life

"And even the very hairs of your head are all numbered" (Matt. 10:30). Have you ever tried to count the number of hairs on your head? Most of us probably tried that when we were children, but we learned quickly that it was a futile exercise. Scientists say the average human head is covered with 100,000 strands of hair. They also tell us that 50 strands fall out each day no matter what we do. Interestingly, the amount of hair varies by color. Blondes have an average of 140,000 strands of hair, brunettes 105,000, and redheads 90,000.

All of this is fascinating trivia, but it's not something I think about often. And when I do think about my hair, it's always in the aggregate: Is it too long? too short? time for a haircut? Is it combed properly? Did I put enough goop on it to keep it in place? I never pick out a strand of hair and say to myself, "I wonder how Number 437 is doing?"[4] I don't number the hairs on my head, but God does. *Our God is a God of the details.* He numbers all the hairs on my head. Think about that for a moment. In my family that would mean . . .

100,000 for me
100,000 for Marlene
100,000 for Josh
100,000 for Mark
100,000 for Nick.

That's a half-million just for my family. In our congregation there are millions of hairs to keep track of, and we're just one church. Our God counts *all* the hairs of *all* his children. Millions and billions of hairs. He numbers them all. The meaning of this is clear: *If God cares for things that matter so little, then he cares for things that matter much more. And if God knows each strand of hair individually, he knows each of us individually as well.* This means that God's knowledge of us is not just general but amazingly specific. He knows us through and through, and he knows us in minute detail. In fact, he knows us far better than we know ourselves.

In his sermon on Matthew 10:30, Charles Spurgeon illustrates God's minute care from the life of Joseph in Genesis 37–50. He points out that there was a "chain of circumstances" that had to happen in a particular way in order for the story to take place as it did. Spurgeon offers a long series of questions: Why did Jacob want to send Joseph? Why were Joseph's brothers on this particular day in a different location? Why did the Ishmaelites come along at that moment? Why were they in the mood to purchase a slave? Why were they going to Egypt and not to some other destination? Why did Potiphar purchase Joseph? Why did his wife have designs on Joseph? Why were the baker and cupbearer in the prison when Joseph was there? Why couldn't Pharaoh remember his dream? Why did the cupbearer remember Joseph? Spurgeon points out that every single one of these seemingly unconnected events had to happen in a particular way at a particular time in order for Joseph to be in the right place at the right time to preserve his family in Egypt during the great famine in Canaan. Spurgeon goes on to say that "God is to be seen in little things." And he uses a lovely phrase to describe all those "random" details. They are the "minutiae of Providence." That's a wonderful way to put it.[5]

After I finished a week of speaking at Dallas Theological Seminary, the president, Mark Bailey, took Marlene and me out for lunch. When he asked where we wanted to go, I said that I didn't want to leave Dallas without having some good barbecue. He laughed and said he knew just the place. While we were driving along North Central Expressway, I commented to Dr. Bailey about a ten-story apartment building that the seminary had just built for married students and also for single women students. When I asked about the millions of dollars it cost to build, Dr. Bailey said that the money had arrived in an unusual way. A friend told the seminary about a young couple who might like to give a significant gift even though they had never given to the seminary before. Eventually the couple made of a gift of several million dollars to the project. When it turned out that the building would cost more than expected, the couple made an additional pledge of more than a million dollars. But there was even more money to be raised. At one point, the situation looked bleak until one of the board members, a man of great faith, said that they should stop worrying and start praying for God's guidance. Soon after that, the money came flowing in.

We pulled into the parking lot of the restaurant just as Dr. Bailey was finishing that story. It was very crowded, so Dr. Bailey said, "We need a parking spot, Lord." And just at that very moment, a car pulled out from a parking space right in front of the main entrance. "Thank you, Lord," Dr. Bailey said. As I thought about that later, I hesitated to mention it because it might seem too trivial. Who knows? Maybe that kind of thing only happens to seminary presidents. But then I ran across this sentence from Spurgeon: "Blessed is that man who seeth God in trifles!" What a positive insight that is. We tend to look at the million-dollar answer to prayer and say, "What a mighty God we serve." *But the God of the large is also the God of the small.* The God who hung the stars in space is also the God who numbers the hairs on your head. Why should it surprise us that God arranges parking spaces when we need them? It is no harder for God to provide something large than something small. After all, they're all "small" to him. (After I mentioned this incident to my congregation, a woman came up and told me she always prays for parking spaces, especially when she is taking her children to visit the doctor. "Mothers with children need to find parking spaces quickly, so I pray for them all the time." Then I received a note from someone who heard that particular sermon and had attended the potluck dinner afterwards. They are fairly new to Calvary and don't know many people. One of our longtime couples sat with them to welcome and encourage them. "You know, Pastor Ray, I had prayed that we would share time with someone at the potluck, and as our heavenly Father cares about the *smallest* detail, he came through." Then she added: "I pray that he blesses your week, especially in the 'minutiae of Providence.'")

F. We Can Encourage Others Who Are Faltering

Hebrews 10:24–25 points us to a crucial ministry of encouragement in light of the Lord's return: "Think of ways to encourage one another to outbursts of love and good deeds. And let us not neglect our meeting together, as some people do, but encourage and warn each other, especially now that the day of his coming back again is drawing near" (NLT). Eugene Peterson translates the first phrase of verse 24 as "Let's see how inventive we can be." Other translations speak of "spurring" other believers on to spiritual growth. How? By a kind word. By a phone call. By a note or an E-mail. By a friendly smile. By a kind word of thanks. And especially by meeting together—in Sunday school and in small groups and in fellowship meetings and at the Lord's Table and in Sunday worship services. Don't be a Lone Ranger Christian. Jesus is coming back! The signs are all around us. *You can encourage other believers by showing up on Sunday morning instead of staying in bed or playing golf or watching TV or walking your dog.* Do those things some other time. In these "end of the world" days, when we see "The Big Day" approaching, let's make sure we come together to worship and to encourage each other. Take time to lift up a fallen brother. Say hello to a discouraged sister. Lift up the arms that have fallen. When a friend falls, pick him up and help him get back in the race for God (see Heb. 12:12–13).

G. We Can Wait Patiently Because We Know the End of the Story

A Southern gospel song says, "I've read the back of the Book and we win!" If you've read Revelation, you know it's

Name three friends who could use some encouragement from you. Beside each name, jot down how you plan to encourage them.

1. _____

2. _____

3. _____

"Dear children, let us not love with words or tongue but with actions and in truth." (1 John 3:18)

true. Jesus wins in the end, and he wins big! *And everyone joined by faith with Jesus wins because he is the Captain of our Salvation.* When the Captain wins, the whole team wins. The forces of evil cannot stand against him. He speaks the word and they are banished forever. Read it for yourself. Jesus wins! The devil loses! And all those on the devil's side lose with him. That includes the demons and every worker of iniquity and all the various ranks of evil spirits and all those who have wittingly or unwittingly done the devil's bidding on the earth.

The problem is, right now we're living in an "in-between" time—when Christ's victory has been secured by his resurrection from the dead, but it has not yet been fully exercised on the earth. The devil fights on even though he is a thoroughly defeated foe. Death still reigns. Christians still suffer and die. And little babies sometimes die. Early one morning I received a call saying that a baby had died in the night and would I please come to the hospital? The baby had been born four months premature and weighed about a pound and a half. He lived twelve days. When I arrived at the hospital, the parents held their precious baby in their arms. Through her tears, the mother said, "There must be a reason for this. God would not do this without a reason." *There is a reason, but the final answer is hidden in the heart and mind of God.* But the faith that leads her to say, "There must be a reason," is truly biblical faith. Even through our tears and when our hearts are broken, we still believe, and because we still believe, we wait patiently for the end of the story to be revealed. James 5:7 instructs us to be patient until the Lord's coming. Verse 8 says, "Be patient and stand firm, because the Lord's coming is near." How precious that truth seems to me as I type these words and think about that little baby who slipped away from us in the middle of the night. Waiting in such circumstances is almost unbearably difficult, but it is infinitely preferable to the alternative, which is to say that there is nothing to wait for, that little babies die for no reason, and we will never see them again because death ends all. I, for one, refuse to embrace such a hopeless philosophy of life. I want a religion that answers the problem of death. *Thank God, we have a hope that goes beyond the grave, a hope that reaches beyond this life to connect us with the life that will never end.* That hope is found in Jesus Christ. Therefore, as Paul said, we do not sorrow as those "who have no hope" (1 Thess. 4:13). And we do not lose heart because the momentary trials of life (what faith it takes to say such a thing!) are far outweighed by the glory that will be revealed in us. The only thing left for us in times of incredible sorrow is to fix our eyes on unseen realities. The undertaker will not have the last word. Better days are coming, and they aren't far away (see 2 Cor. 4:14–16).

"I Am Persuaded"

As we wrap up our study of the Seven Laws of the Spiritual Life, it's good to remember what we know and what we don't know. In this life many things remain a mystery to us, especially the troubling issues of personal loss, sudden death, and unexplained suffering. At the end of the day, after all our thoughts and prayers and meditations, and even after our deep study of the Word of God, we simply don't know why some things happen the way they do. Certainly we could imagine that things might turn out differently if we were in charge of the universe. But that observation leads us right back to the First Law: *He's God and We're Not.* It's amazing how often we come face-to-face with that reality. But the First Law is basic to all the rest. If God is God, he must do many things that are far beyond our understanding. That truth does not answer all our questions, but perhaps it will enable us to quiet our hearts and to sleep at night when otherwise we wouldn't be able to sleep at all.

And the things we know are all-important. Nothing is wasted with the Lord. *Even the parts of life that make no sense to us today will be seen in the light of eternity to have fulfilled God's eternal purpose.* Between now and then, we march onward and upward, moving toward the light that shines brighter and brighter. We march on with faith, hope, and love, with deep confidence in the God who made us and who loved us enough to die for us so that we could be with him. As Paul said in Romans 8:38–39, we are persuaded, we truly believe, we are finally convinced that neither life nor death, nor angels nor principalities nor powers, and nothing above or below or anything else we can encounter in all creation, nothing, absolutely nothing can separate us from the love of God in Christ Jesus our Lord. This we believe. On this truth we have staked our lives. For this we live and for this we will die. In Jesus we have become more than conquerors. Paul said, "I am persuaded" (NKJV). I say to you that I am persuaded. Are you persuaded? Paul was convinced. I am convinced. Are you convinced? Can you truly say, "I no longer have any doubts? I know that God will keep me safe to the very end?" If you are not certain, it is because you are looking to yourself and not to the Lord. Take a good look at Jesus, and you will be convinced. *I am persuaded, and I am glad that I am.*

> *A TRUTH TO REMEMBER:*
> God fully intends to keep his promises to you.
> ✑

What God starts, he finishes. This is the Seventh Law of the Spiritual Life.

GOING DEEPER

1. Reread the Bonhoeffer quote from the first paragraph of this chapter. How does this "very narrow way" work out in your own life?

2. One application of the Seventh Law is that we must wait in hope for the Lord to fulfill his promises to us. Name several ways in which you are waiting on the Lord right now.

3. Do you believe Christ will return in your own lifetime? Why or why not? According to Titus 2:11–14, how should we live while we wait for the return of Christ? Are you personally looking forward to Christ's Second Coming? Are you ready to meet him when he comes?

4. "Even the tragedies of life will fit into God's eternal plan." How do we know this is true?

5. What argument does the author make from Romans 8:29–30 regarding the certainty of our salvation? What is the significance of the fact that "glorified" is in the past tense?

6. If you are studying this book in a group, take time to read Romans 8:31–39 out loud together. Otherwise, take time to read it out loud by yourself. Do you have the same confident assurance as the apostle Paul? Memorize these verses in order to anchor the truth of the Seventh Law deep in your heart.

CHAPTER 8

We Have Come to Shechem

A FEW MILES NORTH OF JERUSALEM, the remains of an ancient city nestle between two mountains. To get there you take a bus ride out of Jerusalem up into the hill country of Samaria. The road is built over an ancient trade route called the Way of the Diviners' Oak. After you have traveled about thirty miles, two mountains appear on the left—Mount Ebal on the north and Mount Gerizim on the south. Between the two mountains a road branches off to the west. If you followed it, you would eventually come to the Mediterranean Sea. Thousands of years ago a city was built between those two mountains. The reason was obvious. The two mountains afforded a degree of protection, and the confluence of two trade routes made it an ideal location for a settlement. That ancient city was called Shechem.

It had a long and important history during the days of the Old Testament. It is mentioned in the Bible as early as Genesis 12, for Shechem was the place where God spoke to

Abraham and promised to give the land of Canaan to his off-spring. Abraham built an altar in Shechem as a reminder of God's promise to him (vv. 6–7). A few years later Abraham's grandson Jacob stopped on his way back from Padan Aram and buried the household idols his wife had stolen. He was on his way back to Bethel to rededicate his life to God. Part of that rededication meant getting rid of the idols, which he buried "under the oak at Shechem" (35:1–4). Several hundred years later, Moses gathered the people of Israel on the eastern bank of the Jordan River to deliver his final message to them. The words he spoke—recorded in the Book of Deuteronomy—were meant to guide the nation as it entered the Promised Land. As he reached the end of his message, Moses gave the people some very specific advice. He warned them to keep the covenant they had made with God, promising blessings if they kept it and curses if they didn't. He specifically told them to build an altar on Mount Ebal. They were to worship God there and to write the Law of God on stones covered with plaster (Deut. 27:4–8).

Soon after that Moses died and Joshua became the leader of the nation. He led the people across the Jordan and into battle at Jericho and Ai. Then he led them north to the plain between Mount Gerizim and Mount Ebal. There he did as Moses had commanded. He built an altar on Mount Ebal and copied the Law of God onto stones covered with plaster. Half of the people stood before Mount Ebal and the other half before Mount Gerizim. Joshua read "the words of the law—the blessings and the curses—just as it is written in the Book of the Law" (Josh. 8:34).

As for Me and My House

There is a certain pattern at work in all these things that took place at Shechem. The pattern is this: Shechem is a place where the words of God were affirmed by the people of God. Abraham affirmed the promise that his offspring would inherit the land; Jacob affirmed the truth that God honors those who worship him in purity; Joshua affirmed the principle that the people of Israel must keep the Law of God. In short, Shechem was a place where—over the centuries—great spiritual decisions were made.

But we haven't yet mentioned the most famous example of all. That took place at the very end of Joshua's life. He—like Moses before him—gave a farewell message. Joshua 24:1 tells us that he "assembled all the tribes of Israel at Shechem." The message that he gave had two parts. *The first part (vv. 2–13) was a recital of the many blessings of God.* Joshua reminded the people how God had given the land to Abraham and his offspring (vv. 2–4), how he had miraculously delivered the nation at the Red Sea (vv. 5–7), how God delivered them from the Amorites and the Moabites (vv. 8–10), and finally, how God had given them the Promised Land in a series of amazing military victories (vv. 11–12). His conclusion was very clear: "So I gave you a land on which you did not toil and cities you did not build; and you live in them and eat from vineyards and olive groves that you did not plant" (v. 13). It was a reminder that what they had was given them by the grace of God. They did not earn it or deserve it.

The second part (vv. 14–24) is a reminder of their obligations before God. They must put away foreign gods once and for all and

197

choose to serve the Lord. That is the background for the well-known words, "As for me and my household, we will serve the LORD" (v. 15). The people responded with enthusiasm that they were ready to do what Joshua was asking of them (vv. 16–18, 21, 22, 24). So Joshua made a covenant for them. That meant he actually wrote down the decrees and laws of God they were promising to keep. He recorded them in the Book of the Law and then he "took a large stone and set it up there under the oak near the holy place of the LORD" (vv. 25–26). Then he added, "This stone will be a witness against us" (v. 27).

The stone was a public symbol of the commitment they were making. Every time the people saw it, they would be reminded of the promise they had made. But God would see the stone as well. It was a reminder to them and to him of the serious commitment made by the nation.

The Hinge of History

Some readers may wonder about the relevance of this bit of biblical history. The answer goes something like this: *Throughout history the people of God have come to crucial moments in which they have reaffirmed their basic commitments.* In those moments, the foundational commitments have been reasserted, and the congregation has publicly agreed to keep them. That is what happened at Shechem for Joshua and the nation of Israel. It wasn't anything new. It was the reaffirmation of what they had already agreed to do. Such moments almost always come at the "hinge" of history, when one era is ending and another one beginning. It might be that a beloved leader is retiring and another one is arising to take his place. It might be that a major redirection of ministry is taking place. It might be that a historic anniversary calls for a public recommitment. The purpose of reaffirming your direction is so that, as you go forward, you don't lose your way altogether.

The Seven Laws of the Spiritual Life by themselves are only words on a piece of paper. You can recite them, study them, memorize them, or put them on a poster you look at each day, but until you decide to make them a part of your life, you will remain as you are.

It's one thing to say you believe the Ten Commandments.

It's something else to live by to the Ten Commandments.

The time for personal commitment always comes sooner or later. The call came from an old friend, someone I have known for more than forty years. His marriage was in serious trouble; but more importantly, he saw clearly that unless he changed from the inside out, what happened to his marriage wouldn't really matter. His wife wasn't the problem, although she has her issues to deal with, and his rocky marriage was only a symptom of deeper problems. "Ray, it's not her fault. She's not the issue; I'm the issue. For a long time I've been struggling with my anger. For the last five years (he was referring to a setback in his professional career) I haven't been able to trust anyone. I've decided that I can't go on this way. A long time ago I had a close relationship with the Lord, but somehow I lost that, and I'd like to get it back. I know that forgiveness is a huge issue in my life, and when I drink, that's when my anger seems to come out, and I end up saying stupid things and hurting my wife." Everything he said was true. Nothing was exaggerated or blown out of proportion.

"I've decided to go see the pastor of the church we've started attending. I don't know him very well, but I think he's a good man. How much should I tell him about our marriage? I'm not trying to hide anything, I don't want to focus on my wife when I've got to deal with my own problems." "Just tell the pastor what you've just told me," I said. "That's all you need to say. You don't need to worry about anything else." Then my friend added this comment: "I know I can't do this alone. I've tried that before. I need some help. I can't keep on doing what I've been doing for all these years."

There is a world of truth in that last statement. Someone who lived in the grip of alcohol abuse shared this definition with me: Insanity is doing the same thing over and over again and expecting different results. That applies to many areas of life and to the debilitating habits of life that keep us from moving forward. Sooner or later there has to be a change. My old friend decided to ditch the insanity of repeating the same old mistakes over and over. There is real hope any time we are willing to pay the price of admitting our weakness and crying out to God for the help we need. A few days later my friend told me that his visit with the pastor had gone well. They had talked for more than an hour and then spent thirty minutes kneeling in prayer together. That was the longest time he had spent on his knees in at least thirty years. I do not know what will happen in his marriage or in his life generally, but I do know this: My friend is right where he needs to be. When we finally stop playing games and start crying out for mercy, the gates of heaven swing open and the delivering hand of God goes to work on our behalf.

Can you remember a time when you made a personal recommitment of your Christian faith? What was the result in your life?

_____

_____

_____

_____

"Therefore, brothers, by the mercies of God, I urge you to present your bodies as a living sacrifice, holy and pleasing to God; this is your spiritual worship." (Romans 12:1, HCSB)

The Truth Will Set You Free but . . .

Several years ago I stumbled across an important spiritual truth after one of my brothers came for a visit. He told me about a counselor he had been seeing who had given him a lot of help. A few weeks later I had the opportunity to visit the counselor myself. He gave me a personality inventory and later mailed the results to me. My brother also sent me some sheets of paper the counselor had given him.

On one page the counselor had done a takeoff on the famous words of Jesus: "You shall know the truth, and the truth shall make you free" (John 8:32, NKJV). He had taken the last phrase and printed it like this: *The truth shall make you free . . . but it will hurt you first.* It startled me, and then it was as if someone had turned on a light above my head. Yes, of course, it makes perfect sense. The truth *will* set you free, but it *will* hurt you first. In a flash I realized why most people have trouble growing spiritually. It's not because we don't know the truth. We've got so much truth it's running out our eyeballs. We hear the truth at church, on the radio, from our friends, from books and tapes and seminars and concerts. And we get it straight from the Bible. That's *not* our problem. If just knowing the truth were all we needed, we'd all be candidates for permanent sainthood.

No, the problem runs deeper than that. We know the truth, but we don't want to let it hurt us, so we deflect it, ignore it, deny it, attack it, argue with it, and in general avoid it in any way we can. Our approach is like a spaceship being attacked by aliens. We put up the force field so we can deflect the incoming bullets of truth. After awhile we get so good at deflection that the truth never gets through to us at all.

We hear the truth—we know the truth—but we deflect the truth so it never gets close enough to hurt. Therefore, we are not set free.

And that's why . . .

We're still angry.

We're still stubborn.

We're still bitter.

We're still greedy.

We're still arrogant.

We're still filled with lust.

We're still self-willed.

We're still unkind.

We refuse to let the truth hurt us!

The truly free people are not those who do whatever they want. Truly free people are those who have dared to let the truth hurt them, and in the process of being hurt, they have been set free. "The truth shall set you free . . . but it will hurt you first." Take some time to think about it.

Now, here's the question: *Are you willing to let the truth hurt you?* Whenever you decide to say yes, the words of Jesus will come true for you, and the truth will at last set you free.

Read Daniel 9:1–19. What specific sins does he confess on behalf of his people? According to verse 18, what is the basis of his hope that God will hear and will forgive?

_____

_____

_____

_____

"If we confess our sins, He is faithful and just to forgive us our sins and to cleanse us from all unrighteousness."
(1 John 1:9, NKJV)

The Man Who Denied God

There are times when we all need a new beginning with God. Sometimes we need a new beginning because of our own sin. Sometimes the circumstances of life have so defeated us that we need a fresh start. Sometimes we feel that hope is gone forever. That means returning to the cross of Jesus Christ, where his blood was shed for our sins. That's why I often say, "Run to the cross!" And not just for the unsaved but for Christians too. We all need the healing that comes from the cross of Jesus Christ. And we need it every day.

Often we wonder if God will take us back. The answer is yes, he'll take you back, but you'll never know until you make that journey on your own. A few months ago I was the guest host on *Open Line*, the question-and-answer program heard nationally on the Moody Broadcasting Network. With about three minutes left in the program, I took one final call. As soon as I heard the man's voice, I knew he was distraught. He proceeded to tell me a story unlike anything I have ever heard before. "I used to be a Christian, but my wife left me for another man. When she told me she was leaving, I got angry and ripped up the Bible in front of her. Then I denied God in the name of the Trinity." His voice broke and he started weeping. "I know it was wrong to do that, but I don't think God will ever take me back. What can I do?"

I glanced at the clock and saw that we had about ninety seconds left in the program. It was a dilemma because this was the kind of call you wish you had a whole hour to discuss. The seconds were ticking away, and I had to say something quickly. "Sir, I don't have much time, so let me tell you this one thing. I know God loves you just the way you are, and he will take you back." "But I ripped up the Bible in front of my wife." "Sir, I know God loves you, and he will take you back." "But I denied God in the name of the Trinity." "God loves you, and he will take you back." The man wept openly as I said those words. Now we were down to the last thirty seconds. "We're almost out of time, so I want you to listen carefully. Your broken heart tells me that God will take you back. The Lord never turns away a broken heart. When this program is over, I want you to get on your knees, put the Bible in front of you, tell the Lord you know the Bible is the Word of God, and ask him to forgive you. And I want you to renounce your denial of faith. Tell the Lord that you know he is God, and ask the Lord Jesus to forgive you. Ask him for a fresh start. If you do that, you will not be turned away." With that, our time ran out and the program was over.

I never heard from the man again. I don't know if he took my counsel or not, but I am sure I told him the truth. No matter how great sin may be, if we turn to the Lord, he will abundantly pardon. "Who is a God like you, who pardons sin and forgives the transgression of the remnant of his inheritance? You do not stay angry forever but delight to show mercy" (Micah 7:18).

Do you know someone (a friend, a coworker, a family member) who has turned away from the Lord? Take a moment and pray for them. Ask God to do whatever it takes to bring them back to him.

"As for me, far be it from me that I should sin against the Lord by failing to pray for you." (1 Samuel 12:23)

A Place to Begin

What should we do if we need a new start with the Lord? Here are four simple answers to that question.

1. Yield Your Memories and Your Dreams to the Lord

Was your past better and happier than your present? Yield it to the Lord. Was your past filled with sadness and pain? Give that to the Lord too. Do you have great dreams, bright hopes, big plans for the future? That's wonderful. It's good to dream big, but in all your dreaming and all your hoping and all your planning, yield it all to the Lord. Lay it at his feet and say, "Your will be done." Take the past with its happiness and sadness, take the future with all its unlimited possibilities—and give it all, past and future, to the Lord who spans the generations. Say to him, "Lord, you are the God of yesterday and you are the God of tomorrow. I yield them both to you so that I may live for your glory today."

2. Accept Your Present Situation as from the Lord

To "accept" does not mean passive resignation to the problems of life. This is not a call to give up and stop fighting for what you believe in. But it does mean accepting the reality that you are where you are right now because this is where God wants you to be, because if God wanted you to be somewhere else, you would be somewhere else. *Only those who have a high view of God can come to this conclusion.* Sometimes you must come to this certainty by a conscious choice of the heart. Blessed is the person who can say, "I am here by the sovereign choice of a loving God, and I know my Lord makes no mistakes." This does not mean it is wrong to change your situation if you need to (and if you can), but it gives you the bedrock confidence that higher hands are at work in your life and that you are being led by the Lord. "Yea, though I walk through the valley of the shadow of death, I will fear no evil: for thou art with me; thy rod and thy staff they comfort me" (Ps. 23:4, KJV).

3. Resolve to Obey God Right Where You Are

Disappointment may cause us to become bitter, and bitterness may make us lethargic toward the duties of life. We may find a thousand excuses not to do the things we know we ought to do.

Little by little things begin to slide: jobs are not done, chores are not finished, projects are left uncompleted, phone calls are not returned, appointments are not met, messages are not answered, papers are not written, goals are not met, and down we slide into a bottomless pit of despair. The answer is so simple that we often miss it. Resolve in your heart that you will obey God right where you are. No excuses. No delays. No hoping for better days, happier times, or more favorable circumstances. If things aren't what you wish they were, roll up your sleeves anyway and go to work. Who knows? Your willingness to do what needs to be done may change the way things are. And even if the situation does not improve, you can hardly make it worse by doing what needs to be done. And if you somehow make it worse, at least you have the satisfaction of knowing that you made it worse by doing your duty, not by giving up and throwing in the towel. "Whatever your hand finds to do, do it with all your might" (Eccles. 9:10a).

4. Praise God for His Goodness in Spite of Your Circumstances

While on an errand to pick up our lawnmower from the repair shop, I happened to tune in while a preacher was talking about the importance of praising the Lord. He made the point (loudly) that praise is a choice, not a feeling. "You aren't supposed to wait until you *feel* like praising the Lord. You're to praise the Lord at all times whether you *feel* like it or not. Many times you won't *feel* like praising the Lord. That doesn't matter. Praise isn't about your feelings. Praise is a choice we make without regard to our feelings." He was exactly right. *Don't wait until the victory is won to praise the Lord.* Stop and praise him before the battle is begun. Then praise him in the midst of the conflict. And praise him even when things seem to be going against you. Praise him for being with you right now. That will put your soul in the right place to continue to work with joy in the days to come.

It is a great advance in the spiritual life if you can praise the Lord even when things are not going well. Ezra 3 tells the story of the relaying of the foundation of the temple in Jerusalem by the Jews who had returned from exile in Babylon. In the midst of the devastation of Jerusalem, with only the foundation of the temple relaid, with rubble on every hand, after returning to find their homeland controlled by their enemies, still the people said with one voice, "[God] is good" (v. 11). That's true faith. Anyone can praise God when the sun in shining, all the bills are paid, your marriage is strong, your kids are doing well, you just got a raise, and the future is bright. It's something else to praise God when things are far from perfect. It's a great thing to be able to look at your life and say, "It's not what I wish it was, but God is still good to me."

Rough Seas Make Great Sailors

Let this be the basis of your thanksgiving. *God's goodness is proved not only in what he gives, but also in what he allows.* Hard times are hard precisely because they force you out of your comfort zone. They put you in a place where you are virtually forced to trust God. They move the spiritual life from theory to reality. You can hear all the sermons you want about how God takes care of his children, but it's not until you experience it for yourself that those truths become the liberating foundation of a life that cannot be blown away by the winds of adversity. Some have said, "Rough seas make great sailors." You can read about sailing until you know all the nautical terms by heart, but you'll never learn how to sail, much less be a great sailor, until you take your turn at the helm while your sailboat fights through a squall off Cape Fear. When the waves are pounding, the wind is howling, and the rain rolls across the deck in horizontal sheets, then you'll learn how to sail and how to survive. If you don't learn at that point, you probably won't make it back to shore. When the storm has passed, you will thank God for the knowledge and confidence that could not have come any other way. There are no shortcuts to spiritual maturity. So give thanks to God even though your circumstances are not the best.

Better to Begin Small

God's grace is so great that, no matter how great our sin, there is always the possibility of a new beginning with him. No matter how checkered your past may be, the grace of God is always greater than your sin. While the scars of the past may be with you forever, those scars do not determine what your future will be. So if you need a new beginning, turn to the Lord with all your heart because he will not turn you away. When we have been humbled by God, our praise will be sweeter because it will be unmixed with sinful pride.

Let's bring the truth home with two statements I would like you to repeat out loud. That's right. Wherever you happen to be right now, I'd like you to say the next two sentences aloud:

It is better to begin small with God than not to begin at all.

It is better to rejoice over what you have than to weep over what you used to have.

Disappointment is a tricky emotion. It's not wrong to remember the past, and it's certainly not wrong to grieve over what you lost. If our loss was caused by our own stupid choices, then grieving may keep us from making the same mistakes again. But eventually there comes a time when we must move on. At that point our beginnings are likely to be small and insignificant. Do not despair. From tiny acorns mighty oaks someday grow. When God wanted to save the world, he started with a baby in a manger. Small beginnings are no hindrance to the Lord. Go ahead and get started. You never know what God will do.

How long are you going to allow your future to be defined by your past? How long will you choose to stay in your disappointment? Don't despise your present because it's not what you wanted it to be or because it's not what your past used to be. Lay your disappointments at the foot of the cross. Let Jesus have them. Take your burdens to the Lord and leave them there. Give thanks for all your blessings. Then by God's grace, move forward with your life, determined to serve the Lord.

A Promise and a Prayer

As we wrap up this book, let's return to the place we started—with a focus on the Lord. The First Law reminds us that everything begins with God, and the Seventh Law teaches us that everything ends with God. In between, which is where we all live during our short life on earth, everything depends on God. True spirituality is

---

Take a two-minute "Praise Break" and give thanks to God for his blessings. Write down three specific reasons you can praise the Lord in your current circumstances.

1. _____

2. _____

3. _____

"Praise the LORD, O my soul, and forget not all his benefits."
(Psalm 103:2)

God-centered in the highest sense of the word. Without God's help, the Seven Laws will never change us or make a difference in the way we live. We must not fall into the self-help trap of thinking everything depends on us. It doesn't. Everything depends on God. If he doesn't help us, we're sunk. But if he does help us, then the Seven Laws can transform our daily life.

Hebrews 13:20–21 is one of the greatest benedictions in the Bible. For many people, a benediction is nothing more than the prayer at the end of a worship service. It's a sign that things are winding up and you can go ahead and gather your Bible and your purse and get ready to leave. But that doesn't apply to the benedictions in the Bible. They are meant to teach us important spiritual truths. Take a moment and read these two verses thoughtfully: "May the God of peace, who through the blood of the eternal covenant brought back from the dead our Lord Jesus, that great Shepherd of the sheep, equip you with everything good for doing his will, and may he work in us what is pleasing to him, through Jesus Christ, to whom be glory for ever and ever. Amen." In just a few words, the writer of Hebrews has

summarized vast realms of Christian truth. I find in this benediction three great principles relevant to our quest to make the
Seven Laws an ongoing reality.

First, God has already done the hard part. That's what verse 20
is all about. It describes the *promise* upon which the *prayer* of
verse 21 rests. The key is in the phrase "the blood of the eternal
covenant." The *blood,* of course, is the blood of the Lord Jesus
Christ. The *covenant* is the promise God made to give his people
new hearts and the forgiveness of sins (Heb. 10:15–18). It is *eternal* because the fulfillment of the promise rests upon God alone.
That is, the eternal covenant means that God is under obligation
to fulfill his promises. He has said what he will do. The covenant
means he will do it! The fact that it is eternal means that its benefits last forever.

Let me put it this way. When Jesus died on the cross, his
blood established the eternal covenant. That is, his blood made it
possible for each of us to have a new heart and the forgiveness of
sins. That's the promise God made. It is *guaranteed* by the blood,
extended by the blood, *purchased* by the blood. And now the
blessings of the covenant are available to all who trust in him.
Therefore—by virtue of his bloody death and victorious resurrection from the dead—God is now a God of peace, and Jesus
Christ has become the great Shepherd of the sheep. That is what
is meant by "God has already done the hard part." He sent his
Son. His Son shed his blood. God raised him from the dead. He
is now exalted in heaven. Now we have peace with God. He is our
shepherd, and we are his sheep.

*Whatever else he asks us to do cannot be as hard as what he has
done for us.* If you think it's hard to raise your children for the

Lord, try rising from the dead. It would be a terrible mistake to view the Seven Laws as something we have to do all by ourselves. No, everything we have to do rests on what the Lord Jesus has already done.

Second, God is willing to equip us from the inside out to do his will. This is the message of verse 21. The word *equip* means "to restore to proper working condition." It means getting an army ready for battle or sewing up a hole in a fishing net or setting an arm that is broken. You "equip" something when you prepare it to be used for its proper purpose. And here's the great part: God is willing to "equip" us to do everything he wants us to do. Let me flip that over. *God will never call us to do something without also and at the same time equipping us to do it.* Never. He simply will not do it.

No doubt many people reading these words face difficult situations. You may be out of money, or you may be out of a job. Perhaps you face surgery very soon. Others face debilitating illness. You may have hard decisions you need to make this week, and you don't know what to do. People you loved and trusted may have turned against you. Your dreams may have crumbled to dust. The future may seem very uncertain. Take this word of cheer: Whatever you have to do this week, God will equip you to do it. No matter how hard the road ahead, God has already started mending your nets and arming you for battle. You don't even have to ask him; he just does it because that's the kind of God he is. He never, never, never, never calls you to any hard task without giving you what you need to get the job done.

An E-mail arrived from a friend with the sad news that her twenty-five-year-old son is slowly dying. She and her husband had known since he was a small child that sooner or later this day would come. First, there was diabetes, then kidney disease, and now the slow degeneration of his eyesight. How does a mother cope with this incredible sadness? "I'm not angry at God; I endured that phase *ad nauseum* years ago, and I don't intend to ever revisit it. But I've been wondering what good can possibly come from this disease and its complications. Romans 8:28 seems trite to me given the enormity of the suffering my child will face." While reading the Book of Joshua, she made a crucial discovery: "I'm keeping a running list of God's commands and His promises in Joshua. I've made an interesting observation from them. In chapters 1–7, for every command God gives, he gives one promise. You pointed out in your sermon that God kept all His promises. I think it's equally important that there is equity between commands and promises. He never asked more of Joshua and the Israelites than He was willing to give. This leads me to believe that in this new family trial, that God won't ask me to do more than He does. And, of course, whatever He chooses to do will be much more magnanimous than anything I'm capable of doing."

There is sorrow in those words, but it is sorrow mixed with gritty faith, the kind that refuses to give up even in the worst moments of life. God gives us what we need, when we need it, and he usually doesn't give it to us in advance. We receive grace to help us in the nick of time (see Heb. 4:16).

Notice how he does it. He works in us from the inside out. Hebrews 13:21 says, "May he work *in us* what is pleasing to him" (italics mine). If we need courage, he works that in us. If we need compassion, he gives it to us. If we need integrity, he builds it in.

If we need wisdom, he imparts the wisdom we need. If we need common sense, he finds a way to give it to us. So many of us look at a difficult situation and pray, "Lord, change my situation." That's not usually God's will. Much more often the difficult situation has come as a means of making us grow spiritually. God often brings difficulty into our lives to deepen our total dependence upon him. When that happens, we ought to pray, "Lord, change me so that I can face this situation." That's a prayer God is pleased to answer.

Third, God's only requirement is that he gets the glory. Notice how the benediction in Hebrews 13 ends. "Through Jesus Christ, to whom be glory for ever and ever. Amen" (v. 21). Various commentators have discussed whether "to whom" refers back to "the God of peace" at the beginning of verse 20 or to "Jesus Christ" at the end of verse 21. It could be either, and it could be both. Either way the point is crystal clear. In all things God must get the glory. He gets the glory in the death of his Son, Jesus Christ. He gets the glory in the blood that established the eternal covenant. He gets the glory in the resurrection of Jesus Christ. *And he must get the glory in the equipping of his people to do his will.* He has done the hard part. He has given us new hearts and forgiven us. He works in us to give us whatever we need to do his will. He equips us to go into battle for him. It all comes from him.

Therefore, no matter how successful we are, it all comes from him.

When we walk together in brotherly love—to God be the glory.

When we exercise Christian care—to God be the glory.

When we raise our children for Jesus Christ—to God be the glory.

215

When we encourage one another—to God be the glory.

When we are salt and light in the world—to God be the glory.

When we cheerfully give of our means—to God be the glory.

When our prayers are answered in amazing ways—to God be the glory.

When we endure suffering and "count it all joy"—to God be the glory.

When we are faithful even until death—to God be the glory.

Let us not be ashamed to say that it all comes from him. Without God's help and his mighty hand undergirding our efforts, everything else would come to nothing.

Finish this prayer: "Father, I pray that you would equip me by your Spirit so that I might be able to _____."

"Now to him who is able to do immeasurably more than all we ask or imagine, according to his power that is at work within us." (Ephesians 3:20)

God's Ways Work!

A friend moved to a distant state because he was enticed by the promise of a better job and a larger income. But as sometimes happens, he got into trouble, made some wrong choices, and fell back into a pattern of sinful behavior that had plagued him in the past. Before long he lost his job and had to move back to Chicago. It was a humbling experience for a man who was used to coming out on top in every situation. What did he learn? For one thing, he learned to be careful about how he prayed. Before he left, he told his accountability group that he was praying that he would stay close to God no matter what the cost. His prayer was answered, but not in the way he expected.

He summed up a second lesson he learned in this simple phrase: "God's will will be done." Then he explained his words:

He is God, and I am not. Our God, who knows the very number of hairs on our heads, has a plan for everything. My biggest liability has been success. I have experienced many successes in my life, and undoubtedly I have noticed in my path that during my most successful times, the time that I spent with the Lord diminished. So I would start to rely on my thoughts instead of his. The results: Wrong and selfish decisions. Have I learned that I am nothing without him? Am I ready to give him all glory and honor for all the work he has done through me, and all the work that he has yet to accomplish? Yes and Yes! I have lost everything, I have nothing, and I am nothing, and I am not somebody. I belong to God, and my life is no longer my own. I don't know what God's will is for me, but I do know what his will is not!

Then he added one final thought, which he called "God has a better plan for me."

I am grateful for what I know about the Lord, and my gratitude and faith is growing because of what I don't know. Only God knows the future. Who am I that I should try to decipher it? Will I live to see tomorrow? Is tomorrow within my control? NO! All I have is today, the next minute, or perhaps the next hour . . . if it is thy will. In asking the Lord for guidance and meditating to listen, I want to be of maximum service to those around me wherever the Lord puts me today. In the words of my eleven-year-old son, "Out of all the gifts the Lord has bestowed upon you, Dad, only one is for you—the

Holy Spirit. All the other gifts the Lord has given you are for everybody else around you to benefit from."

The man's conclusion was simple: "God's ways work; mine don't!"

My friend has learned a valuable lesson that in a sense summarizes everything I have tried to say in this book. God's ways work. They always work, and they never fail. As I have tried to make clear, when we live according to the laws God has established, we encounter the blessings of God even in the midst of heartache and personal difficulty. In an earlier chapter I wrote of the faith of Mike and Betsi Calhoun in the aftermath of their daughter's death in a car accident. While I was writing this chapter, I received a letter Mike wrote to their friends and supporters. Here is part of what he said:

As I wrote the prayer requests for the upcoming months, I did so with a new sense of reality. I am more keenly aware of the fact that God's plan and my best plans, even the prayed over ones, may be different. I have a greater urgency to reach people for Christ. I am more apt to flow with changes, interruptions, and divine appointments than I was nine months ago. Heaven is sweeter; earth is less attractive as my perspective has changed. I have come to a settled resolve that everything I have believed about God is true.

How many of us could say that last sentence with conviction? Through their tears, Mike and Betsi have come to "a settled resolve" about the fundamental issues of life. They have discovered that God can be trusted when all their questions are not answered. This is what it means to say, "He's God and I am not." And strange though it may seem, once we get to that place, we discover a supernatural joy that we never knew before, and we find that beneath us there is a rock labeled "The Peace That Passes All Understanding."

No one knows what the future holds. We live somewhere between yesterday and tomorrow. Egypt is far behind us; the kingdom is yet to come. Meanwhile, we have come to Shechem, the land between the mountains, where God watches as his people say yes all over again to the promises they have already made.

The First Law: *He's God and We're Not.*

The Second Law: *God Doesn't Need Us, but We Desperately Need Him.*

The Third Law: *What God Demands, He Supplies.*

The Fourth Law: *What You Seek, You Find.*

The Fifth Law: *Active Faith Releases God's Power.*

The Sixth Law: *There Is No Growth without Struggle.*

The Seventh Law: *What God Starts, He Finishes.*

Do you believe these things? If so, write the word *Yes* by each statement.

It seems fitting to end with a prayer of personal commitment that the Seven Laws might become the foundation of all that we say and do. If this prayer expresses the desire of your heart, sign your name beneath it. May these words increase your faith in the God whose Word is forever true.

And to God be the glory, forever. Amen!

Heavenly Father, you are the sovereign Lord of all things, and you are the Lord of my life. I praise you because you are God and I am not. Here and now I confess my total dependence upon you for all things. Thank you for the gift of free grace in Jesus Christ. All that you demand and all that I need I find in him. Grant me a grateful heart and a generous spirit toward others. Teach me to seek first your kingdom above all things. Help me to believe so that I might obey even when I do not see all things clearly. Thank you for giving meaning and purpose in the darkest moments of life. I believe that weeping endures for a night but joy comes in the morning. Teach me to rejoice while I wait for the fulfillment of all you have promised. You have not brought me here to leave me alone now. It is only by your grace that I have come this far; by your grace I will go forward. Equip me now to do your will. Bring me to a settled resolve that everything I have believed about God is true. In the strong name of Jesus I pray these things. Amen.

A TRUTH TO REMEMBER:
God never calls you to any hard task without giving you whatever you need to get the job done.

GOING DEEPER

1. How have you seen the Holy Spirit at work in your life, your family, your close friends' lives, or your church?

2. What great thing would you attempt for God if you knew you could not fail?

3. What excuses have you made for not obeying God? What step(s) of obedience do you need to take this week?

4. "God's goodness is proved not only in what he gives, but also in what he allows." What does that statement mean? How have you seen it work in your life?

5. Read Romans 13:10. What person in your life most needs to experience God's love through you?

6. What are the most important spiritual truths you have learned in the last twelve months? Which of the Seven Laws is most challenging to you right now? Why?

Special Note

*I*F YOU WOULD LIKE TO CONTACT THE AUTHOR, you can reach him in the following ways:

By letter: Ray Pritchard
Calvary Memorial Church
931 Lake Street
Oak Park, IL 60301

By E-mail: PastorRay@calvarymemorial.com
Via the Internet: www.calvarymemorial.com

Notes

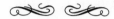

Chapter 1

1. David Maraniss, *When Pride Still Mattered: A Life of Vince Lombardi* (New York: Simon & Schuster, 1999); quote taken from www.jsonline.com.

2. Tony Evans, *Our God Is Awesome* (Chicago: Moody Press, 1994), 89.

3. This quote was spoken by Ravi Zacharias during Moody Bible Institute Founders Week in 2001.

Chapter 2

1. The Lloyd Ogilvie quote was cited by Paul Apple in *A Devotional Commentary on the Psalms,* on-line data file, June 2000.

Chapter 3

1. C. S. Lewis, *Mere Christianity* (Glasgow, Scotland: William Collins Sons & Co., 1952), 123.

Chapter 4

1. Anne Lamott, "Sincere Meditations," www.theooze.com.

2. I have been greatly helped in this area by John Piper's book, *A Hunger for God* (Wheaton, Ill.: Crossway Books, 1997).

Chapter 5

1. Phil Newton, "What Is Faith?" South Woods Baptist Church, Memphis, Tennessee, 2 September 2001.

2. Barbara Winter's quote is found in one of the on-line inspirational collections, for example, www.quoteworld.org and www.thevirtues.org.

3. Philip Yancey, *Disappointment with God* (Grand Rapids: Zondervan, 1988), 201.

Chapter 6

1. Phil Newton, "The Path to Maturity," South Woods Baptist Church, Memphis, Tennessee, 13 February 2000.

2. Mike Huckabee, "Practice of Patience," *Preaching Today,* tape no. 78. Story found on www.preachingtoday.com.

3. Alexander MacLaren, "Patience and Her Work," in *Expositions of Holy Scripture,* vol. 16 (1908; reprint, Grand Rapids: Baker Book House, 1984), 354.

4. William Barclay, *The Letters of James and Peter,* rev. ed. (Philadelphia, Pennsylvania: Westminster Press, 1976), 43.

5. Charles Simeon, "The Duty of Patience," *Expository Outlines on the Whole Bible,* vol. 20 (reprint, Grand Rapids, Michigan: Baker Book House, 1988), 6.

Chapter 7

1. Dietrich Bonhoeffer, "After Ten Years," cited in "Christian Quotations of the Day," April 2002, www.gospelcom.net/cqod/.

2. Peggy Noonan, "The Hard Way," 12 April 2002, www.onlinejournal.com.

3. Ibid.

4. Ken Collins, "Hair Number 437," www.kencollins.com, 11 May 1999.

5. Charles Haddon Spurgeon, "Providence," sermon preached 11 April 1858. Accessed on-line at www.spurgeon.org.